Armies of the Adowa Campaign 1896

The Italian Disaster in Ethiopia

Sean McLachlan • Illustrated by Raffaele Ruggeri

Series editor Martin Windrow

First published in Great Britain in 2011 by Osprey Publishing,
Midland House, West Way, Botley, Oxford, OX2 0PH, UK
44-02 23rd Street, Suite 219, Long Island City, NY 11101, USA

E-mail: **info@ospreypublishing.com**

OSPREY PUBLISHING IS PART OF THE OSPREY GROUP

A CIP catalogue record for this book is available from the British Library

Print ISBN: 978 1 84908 457 4
PDF e-book ISBN: 978 1 84908 458 1
ePub ISBN: 978 1 84908 938 8

Editor: Martin Windrow
Page layout by The Black Spot
Index by Auriol Griffith-Jones
Typeset in Helvetica Neue and ITC New Baskerville
Maps by John Richards
Originated by United Graphic Pte Ltd.
Printed in China through China through World Print Ltd.

11 12 13 14 15 10 9 8 7 6 5 4 3 2 1

Osprey Publishing is supporting the Woodland Trust, the UK's leading woodland
conservation charity, by funding the dedication of trees.

www.ospreypublishing.com

Dedication

For Almudena, my wife, and Julián, my son.

Acknowledgements

This book was made possible by many people, in both Ethiopia
and Italy. Thanks to Abey Seyoum of Abey Roads travel agency for
handling transportation in Ethiopia; to Sntayehu Mekonen
(sntayehu2002et@yahoo.com) for his help as guide and translator;
and to Dr Hiluf Berhe of the University of Axum, for his expert
knowledge of the battlefield and for his continuing work to preserve
this historic site. In Italy, thanks go to military historians and fellow
Osprey authors Pier Paolo Battistelli and Piero Crociani, for their
excellent advice and invaluable help with finding photographs; and
to my superb illustrator Raffaele Ruggeri, who contributed greatly
from his own expert knowledge of this subject.

Author's note

The study of this campaign is hampered by many variant spellings
of the names of places and people. Amharic has its own alphabet,
and European spellings are simply approximations of local
pronunciation. Thus Adowa is often written as Adwa or Adua;
Shewa can be spelt Shoa; and the Treaty of Wuchale can be spelt
Ucciale, Uccialli, or Tog Wajaale. We have used here the most
common spellings found in English-language sources, except in
cases of anglicized personal names: e.g., 'Yohannes' is the Amharic
version of 'John', and we have used the name he actually called
himself. An important note: in many historical and even modern
sources, the Oromo people are referred to as 'Galla'. This term,
given to them by the Shewa, is considered highly offensive, and is
no longer used in Ethiopia except as a term of abuse; we use
'Oromo' throughout.

Artist's note

Glossary

amba	A steep, table-top mountain – a mesa or butte
ascari	Native troops in Italian colonial army; singular, *ascaro*
balambras	Commander of a fortress – one of the lower ranks in the Ethiopian hierarchy of titles of nobility. Above him, in ascending order, were the *dejazmach, kenyazmach, gerazmach, fitawrari, ras* and *negus* (q.q.v.)
buluk	Section of 25 native troops in Italian colonial army
buluk-bashi	Leader of a *buluk*
centuria	Section of 100 men in Italian colonial army
dejazmach	Commander of an Ethiopian rearguard; lit. 'commander of the gate'
fitawrari	Commander of an Ethiopian advanceguard
gerazmach	Commander of an Ethiopian left wing
itegue	Empress
jus-bashi	Native subaltern in Italian colonial army – two per company
kenyazmach	Commander of an Ethiopian right wing
kitet	Ethiopian call to arms
muntaz	Native corporal in Italian colonial army, subordinate to *buluk-bashi*
negus	King – title granted by the *negus negasti* to lords of very high birth and accomplishments
negus negasti	'King of kings' – emperor
ras	Governor of a province
sciumbasci	Native sergeant-major in Italian colonial army
shotel	Curved Ethiopian sword, usually but not invariably sharpened on inside edge of curve
tej	Ethiopian mead (honey wine), often drunk by warriors before battle. Smooth and usually quite strong, it is highly recommended
wagsum	Title used by rulers of Wag and Lasta to show descent from the medieval Zagwé dynasty. This title imparted several symbolic privileges not enjoyed by the typical *ras*
zaptiè	*Ascaro* in the Italian colonial infantry; in practice, *ascaro/ascari* was used for all native soldiers

ARMIES OF THE ADOWA CAMPAIGN 1896

ITALY'S EAST AFRICAN AMBITIONS

A striking portrait of an Eritrean *ascaro*, in this case identified by the badge and light blue tassel on his *tarbush* or fez as serving with the Carabinieri paramilitary police established in the colony. His aspect is typical of fighting men in this part of north-east Africa, whose warrior tradition is undimmed today; the *ascari* proved themselves notably steady under fire. Generally the relationships between Italian officers and their African troops were reported to be good, once new arrivals from Italy had learned the folly of any prejudiced assumptions. There were numerous accounts of *ascari* protecting their officers to the death. (Courtesy Stato Maggiore dell'Esercito, Ufficio Storico – hereafter, SME/US)

In the late 19th century, Italy was one of the youngest of the European nations. It had only been politically unified under the northern throne of Savoy – by force of arms – in 1861, and in human terms this unity was a fiction. Governments anxious to create a true sense of nationhood sought foreign quarrels, in the hope that war – any war – would unite Italians psychologically. Naturally, Italy lagged far behind in the race for colonies, and older and stronger powers such as Britain, France and Spain had already staked claims over much of the non-European world. One of the few remaining regions where Italy might prove itself by gaining colonies of its own was north-east Africa, on the western shore of the Red Sea.

While the French had established a foothold at what is now Djibouti, and the British were expanding their colony in present-day Kenya and Uganda, a large region remained uncolonized – Abyssinia, today known as Ethiopia and Eritrea. This vast territory included high, arid mountains and fertile valleys, as well as peripheral regions of desert and savannah. A patchwork of different tribes inhabited these territories, ruled by a complex aristocratic hierarchy, and to a great extent following an idiosyncratic version of Christianity. Over all was the nominal ruler of the entire country – the *Negus Negasti* or 'king of kings'. Some of these emperors had managed to unify the country for a short time, but under weaker central rulers Abyssinia was a conglomeration of feudal warlord fiefdoms, and this potentially rich but divided land attracted the ambitions of the Italians.

In 1869 the Suez Canal was opened, thus greatly increasing the importance of the Red Sea for the shipping of the far-flung British and French empires. That same year an Italian firm established a coaling station on land bought from a local ruler in Assab Bay, in the narrows of the Gulf of Aden. In 1883 they sold it to the Italian government, which began expanding it into a colony. In 1885, taking advantage of Britain's and Egypt's distraction by the Mahdi's warlike followers in the Sudan (the so-called Dervishes), Italy took possession of the nearby port of Beilul. In the same year the Italians also landed some 250 miles north-westwards up the Red Sea coast and occupied Massawa – one of the most important harbours in the whole region. The Egyptians who had previously claimed it could do little but complain about this landing; their own garrisons would have been unable to hold out against the Mahdi, and Britain approved the transfer of power.

During the following year, Italy spread out along 650 miles of coastline, from Cape Kasar in the north to the French enclave of Obok (modern Djibouti) in the south; this corresponds almost exactly to the coast of

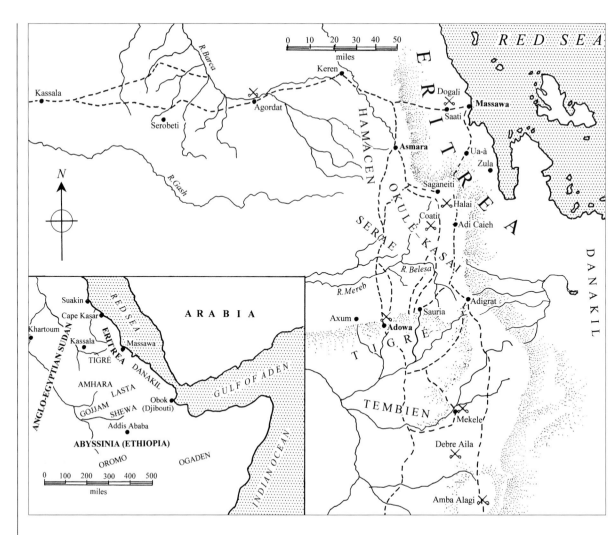

The Mahdist and Ethiopian campaigns, 1885–96; broken lines indicate main Italian lines of communication, and shading shows the approximate edges of the highlands. The provinces of Hamacen, Okule-Kasai and Serae were all historically subject to the rulers of the Tigré region of northern Abyssinia. (Inset) General map of the region. (Maps by John Richards)

modern Eritrea. The British actually encouraged Italian expansion in the Red Sea as a way to offset potential French influence. (While Britain had sent an expedition into Ethiopia in 1868 to defeat the Emperor Tewedros and save his European hostages, they had no interest in actually colonizing the country.)

Defeat at Dogali, 1887

The Emperor Yohannes IV of Ethiopia resented being cut off from the sea by this new Italian incursion. Tensions arose, especially in 1887, when the Italians decided to strengthen their position by pushing inland and taking over the villages of Ua-à and Zula. The local lord, Ras Alula, demanded that the Italians leave, and when they failed to do so he gathered 25,000 warriors. On 25 January 1887 he attacked the fort at Saati, held by 167 Italians and 1,000 native troops, but found it too strong to take. He had better luck the next day, when he attacked a relief column heading for the fort. Led by LtCol De Cristoforis, this force consisted of 500 Italians, 50 native irregulars, and two machine guns. Ras Alula ambushed them at Dogali with about 10,000 warriors; the Italian machine guns soon jammed, and the relief force was surrounded and cut down. The Italians lost 23 officers and 407 men killed, one officer and 81 men wounded. The Italians estimated that Ras Alula lost 1,000 warriors at the battle of Dogali, although this is debatable. The Italians quickly vacated the contested villages, as well as the fort at Saati.

This defeat led to a massive Italian reinforcement of what would become their colony of Eritrea. By the end of 1887 troops in the colony numbered 18,000, of whom only 2,000 were natives, and an arms embargo on Ethiopia was in place. The military governor, Gen Di San Marzano, fortified Massawa, retook the inland villages and fort, and began building more forts on the border and at key internal sites. He also started building a railway from Massawa to Saati, to exploit the region's mineral wealth.

By the end of March 1888, the Emperor Yohannes and Ras Alula were negotiating peace with the Italians. The colony continued to strengthen and expand, and in October 1888 the first units of *ascari* were formed. These native battalions were mostly drawn from the Eritrean population, along with Sudanese gunners, and they replaced the irregular Turkish and local mercenaries that the Italians had previously employed.

The Italians' next challenge came from the loosely structured Mahdiyya army in the Sudan. The Mahdi claimed to be the new prophet of Islam, and his devout followers drawn from disparate peoples made great gains against the British-sponsored Egyptians and neighbouring tribes. There had been a longstanding rivalry between these Muslim warriors and the mostly Christian Ethiopians. Emperor Yohannes campaigned against the Dervishes, but, while at first successful, he was defeated and fatally wounded at the battle of Metemma on 9 March 1889. The Italians took advantage of Yohannes' absence on campaign to push further inland, taking the Tigréan provinces of Hamacen, Okule-Kasai, and Serae; these would become the principal territories of the future colony, and modern nation, of Eritrea.

On his deathbed, Yohannes declared his nephew Ras Mangasha as his 'natural son' and successor, but Mangasha faced powerful rivals for the throne. The most prominent was Menelik of Shewa – the region surrounding the capital, Addis Ababa – who had stayed neutral in the struggle between Yohannes and the Italians in return for Italian guns. Ruling over the populous and fertile central part of the country, Menelik had tens of thousands of warriors at his command, and was already in secret negotiations with the Italians to consolidate his political position. When Yohannes named Ras Mangasha as his heir, Menelik proclaimed himself Negus Negasti on 26 March 1889. The Italians supported Menelik, and on 2 May 1889 the two parties signed the Treaty of Wuchale. This recognized Menelik II as emperor, while in return Menelik conceded most of the land that Italy had already occupied. The treaty also declared a permanent friendship

The *Negus Negasti* Menelik II and his high command, in an engraving made at about the time of the battle of Adowa. While these men wear lion's-mane headdresses and elaborately embroidered silk robes, and carry decorated shields, note that they are armed with rifles. Before March 1896 the Italians often mistook Ethiopian adherence to tradition for an inability to embrace useful technologies. (Courtesy SME/US)

Estimate of Ethiopian military capabilities by province, 1887				
Province	Foot	Horse	of which, with firearms	of which, breech-loaders
Amhara	25,000	10,000	20,000	10,000
Tigré	16,000	4,000	15,000	8,000
Gojjam	12,000	8,000	11,000	2,000
Shewa	35,000	35,000	25,000	8,000

Totals: 145,000 men, of whom 57,000 mounted and 71,000 having firearms; of the latter, 28,000 having breech-loaders. (Source: A. Cecchi, *L'Abissinia settentrionale*, 1887)

Note:
Gun owners who did not have breech-loaders were armed with muzzle-loaders, even flintlocks. However, by 1896 there were many more firearms in the country, the new acquisitions being almost exclusively breech-loaders.

between the two parties, and set up trade connections. However, one contentious clause guaranteed that this treaty would eventually fail. Article 17 stated, in the Italian version, that Italy would control Ethiopia's external affairs; the Amharic version said that Menelik could choose whether or not to ask the Italians to act on his behalf, but was not required to do so. It is unclear why the wording was different; the Ethiopians said it was a trick, while the Italians blamed the Ethiopian translator.

Whoever was to blame, Article 17 soon caused trouble. When Menelik sent letters to England and Germany announcing his accession to the throne, he was told that since the Italians controlled Ethiopia's foreign affairs these messages should have gone through them. He wrote in protest to King Umberto of Italy, and when he failed to get satisfaction he openly renounced the treaty in February 1893.

CHRONOLOGY

1883 Italian government buys Assab Bay from Italian commercial firm
1885 5 February, Italian landing to occupy Massawa
1887
26 January Following ocupation of Ua-à and Zula, Italians suffer 512 casualties in defeat at Dogali
1888 October: first Italian colonial *ascari* units formed
1889
9 March Emperor Yohannes IV fatally wounded in battle of Metemma against Mahdists, and names Ras Mangasha his heir
26 March Menelik of Shewa declares himself emperor
2 May Treaty of Wuchale between Italians and Menelik
3 August Italians occupy Asmara
1890
1 January Italians formally establish colony of Eritrea
March Menelik receives submission of Ras Mangasha and Ras Alula; other chiefs soon follow
27 June Italian troops defeat Sudanese Mahdist force in first engagement at Agordat

1891 1 November, MajGen Oreste Baratieri appointed commander of Italy's African forces
1892
22 February Baratieri appointed civil governor of Eritrea colony in addition to his military role
26 June Italian troops defeat Mahdist raiders at Serobeti
1893
27 February Menelik renounces Treaty of Wuchale
21 December Italians defeat Mahdists in second battle of Agordat
1894
17 July Italians defeat Mahdists at Kassala
18 December Italians relieve Halai fort in Tigré province
1895
13 January Italians defeat Ras Mangasha of Tigré at battle of Coatit
25–28 March Italians fortify Adigrat and Mekele
17 September Menelik calls for total mobilization of Ethiopian forces
9 October Italians defeat Ras Mangasha at Debre Aila
7 December Ethiopians wipe out Italian garrison at Amba Alagi
1896
20 January Italian garrison at Mekele surrenders on terms
14 February Menelik arrives at Adowa, and learns that Baratieri's army is at Sauria
29 February Menelik decides to leave the next day; Baratieri decides to advance that night
1 March Destruction of Baratieri's army in battle of Adowa
10 March Italian government of Francesco Crispi falls
26 October Treaty of Addis Ababa

THE MAHDIST CHALLENGE, 1890–94

The Mahdists fought the Italians for the first time at Agordat on 27 June 1890. About 1,000 warriors raided the Beni Amer, a tribe under Italian protection, and then went on to the wells at Agordat, on the road between the Sudan and northern Eritrea. An Italian force of two ascari companies surprised and routed them; Italian losses were only three killed and eight wounded, while the Mahdists lost about 250 dead. In 1892 the Mahdists raided again, and on 26 June a force of 120 ascari and about 200 allied Baria warriors beat them at Serobeti. Again, Italian losses were minimal – three killed and ten wounded – while the raiders lost about 100 dead and wounded out of a total of some 1,000 men. Twice the ascari had shown solid discipline while facing a larger force, and had emerged victorious. The inferior weaponry and fire discipline of the Mahdists played a large part in these defeats.

Major-General Oreste Baratieri took over as military commander of Italian forces in Africa on 1 November 1891, and also became civil governor of the colony on 22 February 1892. Baratieri had fought under Garibaldi during the wars of Italian unification, and was one of the most respected Italian generals of his time. He instituted a series of civil and military reforms to make the colony more efficient and its garrison effective. The latter was established by royal decree on 11 December 1892. The Italian troops included a battalion of Cacciatori (light infantry),

Ras Mangasha Yohannes, the nephew and designated heir to the Emperor Yohannes IV. Although superseded by Menelik, he remained an influential leader in the Tigré region. Photographed *c.*1894, he wears a richly decorated *lembd* over a silk shirt-tunic, and rides a horse with elaborate silver-decorated tack. Again, he carries both a traditional conical shield and a modern bolt-action rifle – compare with Plate A1. (Courtesy SME/US)

a section of artillery artificers, a medical section, and a section of engineers. The main force was to be four native infantry battalions, two squadrons of native cavalry, and two mountain batteries. There were also mixed Italian/native contingents that included one company each of gunners, engineers and commissariat. This made a grand total of 6,561 men, of whom 2,115 were Italians. Facing the Mahdists, and with tension increasing with the Ethiopians, this garrison was soon strengthened by the addition of seven battalions, three of which were Italian volunteers (forming new 1st, 2nd and 3rd Inf Bns) and four of local ascari, plus another native battery. A Native Mobile Militia of 1,500 was also recruited, the best of them being encouraged to join the regular units. Like all the other colonial powers, the Italians also made widespread use of native irregulars recruited and led by local chiefs.

The first big test came at the second battle of Agordat on 21 December 1893. A force of about 12,000 Mahdists, including some 600 elite Baqqara cavalry, headed south out of the Sudan towards Agordat and the Italian colony. Facing them were 42 Italian officers and 23 Italian other ranks, 2,106 ascari, and eight mountain guns. The Italian force anchored itself on either side of the fort at Agordat, and from this strong position they repelled a mass attack, though not without significant losses – four Italians and 104 ascari killed, three Italians and 121 ascari wounded. The Mahdists lost about 2,000 killed and wounded, and 180 captured.

When the Mahdists launched raids across the border in the spring of 1894, the Italians decided to take the offensive and capture Kassala, an important Mahdist town. General Baratieri led 56 Italian officers and 41 Italian other ranks, along with 2,526 ascari and two mountain guns. At Kassala on 17 July they clashed with about 2,000 Mahdist infantry and 600 Baqqara cavalry. The Italians formed two squares, which inflicted heavy losses on the mass attacks by the Mahdists, before an Italian counter-attack ended the battle. The Italians suffered an officer and 27 men killed, and two native NCOs and 39 men wounded; Mahdist casualties numbered 1,400 dead and wounded – a majority of their force. The Italians also captured 52 flags, some 600 rifles, 50 pistols, two cannons, 59 horses, and 175 cattle. This crushing defeat stopped Mahdist incursions for more than a year, and earned Baratieri acclaim at home. (In 1896 the Mahdi's followers would make several more incursions into Eritrean territory, but without success. Fighting the Italians seriously weakened the Mahdiyya, and contributed to its defeat at the hands of Kitchener's Anglo-Egyptian army at Omdurman in 1898.)

Proxy war in Tigré, 1890–94

While the Italians enjoyed success against the Mahdists, more trouble was brewing with the Ethiopians. The Italians continued to push inland and consolidate their control, causing friction with the inhabitants. On 3 August 1889, Italy had occupied Asmara, the capital of Hamacen province. This had been ruled by Ras Mangasha, Yohannes' nephew who had lost the imperial succession to Menelik. Menelik and the Italians

agreed to divide the Tigré region between them, and they invaded on both fronts in January 1890. The Italians proclaimed the colony of Eritrea on 1 January, providing it with a civil government in addition to the military force. In March, Menelik received the submission of Ras Mangasha and of Ras Alula, Ethiopia's most capable military leader, and the other Tigréan chiefs soon fell into line.

Menelik treated Ras Mangasha with care, since he could use him: the emperor offered Mangasha the crown of Tigré if he could reconquer the parts of that region lost to the Italians. Mangasha duly returned to Tigré and plotted a rebellion; while pretending to be friendly towards the Italians, he called for a general mobilization under the pretence of fighting the Mahdists. On 15 December 1894 he was forced to show his hand when Batha Agos, chief of Okule-Kasai province in northern Tigré, rebelled against the Italians. General Baratieri sent Maj Toselli with 1,500 men and two guns from Asmara to Saganeiti, capital of Okule-Kasai. On 18 December, Toselli discovered that the chief and his force of 1,600 warriors were besieging the small Italian fort of Halai, garrisoned by a company of 220 men. Batha Agos' men had almost taken the fort when Toselli hit them from the rear; the chief was killed, and his army disintegrated. The Italians lost 11 killed and 22 wounded.

General Baratieri now took personal command of a march against Ras Mangasha. On 28 December he camped near Adowa, an important religious and economic centre with a population of about 15,000. This town is at a junction of four roads, leading west to Axum and Gonder, north to Asmara and Massawa, east to Adigrat, and south to Mekele, the capital of Tigré and former seat of the Emperor Yohannes. There, Baratieri received the submission of several chiefs as well as clergy, but Mangasha still threatened his lines of communication and supply. Baratieri withdrew from Adowa, and after much manoeuvring on both sides the armies clashed on 13 January 1895 at Coatit. The Italian force numbered 3,883 men – three ascari battalions of about 1,100 each, 66 Italian officers and 105 Italian rankers, 400 local irregulars, 28 ascari lancers, and four mountain guns. Ras Mangasha had 12,000 men with firearms and 7,000 with swords and spears, but an estimated one-third to a half of their firearms were antiquated muzzle-loaders.

The battle of Coatit

The terrain was typical of the region – rough and broken, with sheer mountains and steep gorges dividing the field. At dawn on 13 January 1895 the Italians advanced, and bombarded the Ethiopian camp with artillery. The Ethiopians were surprised, but soon got in order, and attacked. The ascari stood off aggressive charges by superior numbers, and then pushed forward, alternating steady volleys with bayonet charges. Ras Mangasha put pressure on the irregulars holding the Italian left, and at one stage this forced the entire line to give up all the ground they had gained; but in the event the new Italian position proved stronger, and successive Ethiopian attacks withered under orderly fire. After a few hours the Ethiopians broke off; the following day saw some half-hearted attacks before Mangasha withdrew that night. The Italians pursued for 25 miles before coming upon the Tigréan camp late on 15 January. Again they bombarded it and the Ethiopians slipped away under cover of darkness, leaving behind much equipment.

This victory cost the Italians three officers and 92 men killed, and two officers and 227 men wounded, while the Ethiopians lost an estimated 1,500 killed and about twice that number wounded. The victory at Coatit buoyed Italian confidence, and led to dangerous miscalculations about their own and their enemy's abilities. At that time colonial adventures seemed attractive to many politicians, as a national distraction from economic recession, a financial crisis, and widespread civil unrest. (In 1894 the government of Francesco Crispi had had to send no fewer than 40,000 troops to pacify Sicily, and there was also trouble in central Italy and as far north as the Po valley.)

This proxy war between Menelik's catspaw Ras Mangasha and the Italians did nothing to lessen their mutual hostility. The Italians tried to make allies among Menelik's nobility, hoping to take advantage of the incessant political infighting for which Ethiopia (like Italy) was notorious. They were in regular contact with nearly all the key players, but to no avail; some of the aristocrats shared these messages with Menelik, and together they plotted how best to trick the Italians. The Italians failed to realize that Menelik's reorganized system of government benefitted all of the aristocracy, instead of just one tribe over the rest. Menelik never demanded the annual tribute to which he was entitled from the northern princes, precisely because he wanted them loyal in case of an Italian advance. His centralized taxation system anyway brought him in greater riches than any emperor in recent memory, making him a good man to follow.

Matters were quickly coming to a head when, in March 1895, Baratieri fortified Adigrat and Mekele, two important towns on the roads between the coast and the interior. Baratieri even pushed as far as Adowa once more. He wanted to go further, but the nearly bankrupt government in Rome refused him the funding for such an extended line. Baratieri complained that he could not do his job without more money. He sensed that Menelik was preparing for war, and on three occasions in 1895 he sent in his resignation. Rome refused to accept it, and finally caved in and increased his funding – although not by enough.

CONFRONTATION WITH ETHIOPIA, 1895–96

Baratieri's foreboding was well founded, and on 17 September 1895 Menelik called for general mobilization. Thousands of warriors converged on four regional assembly points, and of these about 35,000 gathered under Menelik himself. His empress Itegue Taitu also mobilized another 6,000. The rest were raised by governors and regional princes, the largest contingent being that of Menelik's cousin Ras Mekonnen of Harar, who brought about 12,000 men. The exact size of the Ethiopian army is unknown; estimates range between 80,000 and 120,000, and at least 100,000 seems probable.

On 9 October 1895, Baratieri led a large Italian force 80 miles south from Adigrat to attack Ras Mangasha at Debre Aila. It was one of the rare instances when the Italians outnumbered the Ethiopians: Baratieri had 116 Italian officers, 672 Italian other ranks, 8,065 ascari, a few hundred militia and irregulars, and ten mountain guns, while Mangasha had only 4,000–5,000 warriors. The Italians lost 11 killed and 30 wounded, the Ethiopians 30 killed, 100 wounded, and 200 prisoners. Far from being cowed by the Italians' superiority, one of the prisoners gave this ominous warning: 'For the moment you have been victorious, because God so willed it; but wait a month or two, and you will see the soldiers of Menelik. They are as many in number as the locusts.'

The Italians, too, were shipping in major reinforcements to deal with the situation. Between 25 December 1895 and 10 March 1896 they landed 1,537 officers, 38,063 men, 8,584 mules, and 100,000 barrels of supplies. Unfortunately for Baratieri, most of them landed only after he had marched into Tigré to confront Menelik, at the head of some 14,000 men (for his order of battle, see 'The Italian Army', below).

The Ethiopians' own march towards the arena of battle was a long one even by their standards, requiring some groups to walk for 150 days over rough and often trackless terrain. On one route the men had to cross the loops of the same serpentine river 28 times. Much of the region had suffered from rinderpest (a deadly cattle disease) and drought, so Menelik set up food depots along the way to reduce the amount of foraging the army had to do. Typically of Ethiopian strategy, Menelik's aim was to defeat the main Italian army, leaving smaller detachments to be mopped up later. When his vanguard came across Maj Pietro Toselli with 1,800 men and four mountain guns dug in at Amba Alagi, it simply bypassed them; Toselli's force was too small to threaten the Ethiopians' rear.

Amba Alagi and Mekele

Fatally for Toselli, however, two Ethiopian commanders found the temptation to strike the first blow irresistible. The Fitawrari Gebeyehu and the Gerazmach Tafese attacked the Italian position at Amba Alagi on 7 December 1895, and this assault attracted all the nearby warriors into the fray – some 30,000 men, including the commands of Ras Mekonnen and

Major-General Oreste Baratieri had fought as a Redshirt under Garibaldi in the war of Italian unification, and also participated in the brief and unsuccessful campaign against Austria in 1866. Nearly three decades later, his consolidation of control over Eritrea and his victories over the Mahdists and Ethiopians earned him an exaggerated reputation at home, but his career ended after the disaster at Adowa. It is said that he lost his *pince-nez* spectacles during the rout and, almost blind, had to have his horse led during the retreat. (Courtesy SME/US)

Ras Mangasha. Together they completely overwhelmed the Italians, who suffered 19 Italian officers (including Maj Toselli), 20 Italian other ranks, and 1,500 ascari killed, and three officers and 300 ascari wounded. The survivors fled some 35 miles north to the town and fort at Mekele, and the rest of the region was abandoned. The Ethiopians suffered an estimated 3,000 casualties; the two impulsive commanders were detained for disobeying orders, but once Menelik arrived on the scene he forgave them. (Had the battle not been such a total victory, their fate might have been much worse.)

Soon the advancing Ethiopian army reached Mekele; such an important fort could not be bypassed, and the vanguard surrounded it. The garrison consisted of 20 Italian officers, 13 Italian NCOs, 150 Italian privates, 1,000 ascari, and two mountain guns. A two-week siege ensued, during which the Ethiopian artillery proved to have a longer range than the Italian guns – 4,900 yards, as opposed to 4,200. The fort was systematically pounded, but frontal assaults proved costly and fruitless; outside the walls the Italians had laid barbed wire, and fields of sharpened stakes and broken bottles to discourage the bare-footed Ethiopians. The defenders shot off signal flares, and sent up an observation balloon to scare the 'savages'; the Ethiopians were duly impressed, but reasoned that since these technological wonders did them no harm, they were of no importance. The siege continued.

Finally the attackers managed to cut off the fort's water supply, and the Italian commander offered to surrender if the garrison could leave bearing their arms. Menelik agreed to these generous terms, both because he wanted to free up his army to march on, and because he could see a use for the prisoners. Ras Mekonnen was sent to 'escort' them back to Italian lines – a convenient way to bring a major part of the Ethiopian army deep into Italian-held territory without being molested.

The main Ethiopian force followed, avoiding the strong Italian fort at Adigrat and moving on to Adowa on 14 February 1896. They found the Italians dug into a strong position at Sauria, 16 miles to the east, with their flanks guarded by almost impassable terrain. Menelik decided not to attack, hoping instead to lure the Italians onto more favourable ground where the superior Ethiopian numbers could be used to full effect.

The waiting game

There now followed a two-week pause in activity by both sides. Withdrawal would have meant a severe loss of face for either commander, and would probably have ended the campaign without a decision. An Ethiopian army, consisting of levies commanded by regional leaders with their own agendas, had to be used before it simply broke up and drifted apart. The Italian army had a series of recent defeats on its record, and Baratieri was receiving strident cables from Rome insisting on a decisive victory (Prime Minister Crispi had wanted to replace Baratieri, but the general was saved by the support of King Umberto). The Italian commander had exuded confidence before the campaign, thinking that Menelik could gather at most 60,000 men – a force that the Italians could probably have dealt with, given their strong position. But when twice that number showed up, Baratieri's position became hazardous, and his previous boasts came back to goad him.

On 29 February (1896 being a leap year), Menelik could wait no longer. His supplies were nearly exhausted, and he decided that a small victory would be better than none. He announced that the next day he would lead his army around the Italians and north into the province of Hamacen, which included Asmara, now the seat of the colonial government in Eritrea. He apparently intended to ravage the countryside, and perhaps to strike at Asmara before withdrawing.

In one of the ironies of military history, that very night Gen Baratieri – who favoured a temporary withdrawal – was persuaded both by the unanimous advice of his brigade commanders, and by constant pressure from Rome, to order an advance. His army, too, had only a few days' supplies left, and spies informed him that much of the Ethiopian army had scattered across the countryside foraging, or were praying in various churches around Adowa in preparation for a feast day on 1 March. These reports were exaggerated, either by mistake or design. While some warriors were indeed foraging or praying, most had not strayed far; and in any case, the Ethiopian numbers were such that, even with part of the force absent, they still outnumbered the Italians by a factor of anything between 4:1 and 8:1.

Photo of part of the defences of the Italian fort at Adigrat. Built in March 1895 as a base for operations in Tigré, this had to be abandoned under the peace terms agreed a year later after the battle of Adowa. (Piero Crociani Collection)

ADOWA: THE ITALIAN ADVANCE

About 7 miles east of Adowa, and rather less than 4 miles from the Ethiopian advance camp in the valley of Mariam Shavitu, a series of towering mountains are divided by narrow valleys: from the north, Mt Eshasho, Rebbi Arienni and Mt Raio, with to the south-west of them the Spur of Belah, the Hill of Belah, Mt Belah, and to the south Mount Kaulos and Mt Semaiata. Across a couple of miles of lower but still very rolling and difficult ground to the west of them is another line of heights: Mt Nasraui, Mt Gusoso, and Mt Enda Kidane. These look down to both the north and west into the hooked valley of Mariam Shavitu, and south-west towards Adowa town (see map, page 16). Baratieri decided to advance westwards to these twin chains of mountains and challenge the Ethiopians to battle; if he threatened the important town of Adowa, Menelik would have to respond. While the Italian position would not be as strong as at Sauria, the mountains should still offer the Italians protection from flanking movements.

However, for Baratieri to bring his force to the designated objectives was fraught with difficulties. His men would have to march by night in three separate columns, and get into position before dawn in order to achieve surprise. Baratieri's maps were sketchy and inaccurate, and his local scouts were not as familiar with the terrain as they claimed, while some were actually spies for Menelik. One observer commented that the camp at Sauria was wide open; Ethiopian civilians came and went at will, selling goods and services to the soldiers. However, while Menelik certainly had a thorough knowledge of the Italians' numbers, his informants did not have time to report the last-minute Italian advance.

The Italian force got on the march at 9pm on the evening of 29 February. Generals Albertone, Arimondi, and Dabormida led three separate columns – respectively, the Native Brigade, 1st and 2nd Infantry Brigades – while Gen Ellena's 3rd Infantry Brigade followed Arimondi's as rearguard and reserve. Their first objective was Rebbi Arienni, part of the eastern chain of mountains situated just over 7 miles short of Adowa; Baratieri intended to fight in this first line of heights, and, if things went well, to advance to the western hills within sight of the town.

While the weather was fair, the night march was difficult. The terrain in this region is extremely rough, with steep, at times sheer mountains and hills rising up everywhere, separated by narrow valleys and streams. At that time roads were nonexistent, and the soldiers had to take narrow, winding footpaths. While the terrain is rugged, the valleys are fertile, and the Italians passed numerous farms on the way; the country was full of eyes.

The Italian columns inevitably 'concertina'd', like any file of men moving across rough terrain, especially by night, and the brigades soon found themselves getting mixed up. Dabormida's rear battalion went too far to the left, and ended up behind Arimondi's. This mistake was soon corrected, but several times Baratieri had to order one column or another to close up as units got separated in the dark. Even worse, Arimondi had to stop for more than an hour as Gen Albertone's troops filed past him; Albertone was supposed to have been on a different path on the left (south).

After getting back on his proper path, Albertone forged ahead; but he ended up in the wrong position, well ahead and to the left of the rest of the

Giuseppe Arimondi, photographed when he was a lieutenant-colonel. Promoted major-general in February 1894, he would be killed at the battle of Adowa two years later while commanding the 1st Infantry Bde and the Italian centre column. (Piero Crociani Collection)

**Major-General Giuseppe Ellena, who commanded the reserve 3rd Infantry Bde, was the most recent arrival of the five Italian generals at Adowa.
He would assist Gen Baratieri in conducting the subsequent retreat northwards by the survivors of his and Arimondi's brigades. (Courtesy SME/US)**

force, and this ruined Baratieri's plan of battle. Baratieri had wanted Albertone to occupy a flat-topped hill south of the left flank of Mt Belah, which would constitute the army's forward position. Baratieri thought this hill was called Kidane Meret, but actually it does not have a name. There is a mountain called Enda Kidane 4 miles further on, with a smaller feature north of it – which is the height that any local would point to if asked for the location of the 'Hill of Kidane Meret'. Albertone probably thought that the hill he first reached soon after 3am on 1 March was Baratieri's 'Kidane Meret'; but after waiting for about an hour, and not seeing Arimondi coming into line on his right as he expected, he started to mistrust his own instincts. (Arimondi, of course, had been badly delayed by the obstruction of the track by Albertone's own brigade.) Albertone's guides insisted that they had not yet reached Kidane Meret; so he followed their lead and advanced. When he halted, he was isolated well to the south-west of the rest of the army, at the Hill of Enda Kidane Meret – the 'real' Kidane Meret. In the western chain of mountains, this overlooks the Mariam Shavitu valley containing Adowa; perhaps Albertone convinced himself that Baratieri wanted him to threaten the town.

Meanwhile, the other two columns were slowly getting into their designated positions in the eastern chain of mountains. Dabormida's brigade arrived at Rebbi Arienni by 5.15am on 1 March. Fifteen minutes later, Arimondi began to occupy the eastern slope of this same height, and to extend his line all the way down to Mount Raio, thus forming the Italian centre. Ellena's reserve column was massed close behind Dabormida in the Hollow of Gundapta.

If Albertone's brigade had been where they should have been, the Italians would have been in a strong position, covering the gaps in the first row of mountains from Mt Eshasho down to the ground south of Mts Belah and Raio. The brigades would have been divided, but safe from flanking manoeuvres, since the mountains – though high, steep, and difficult to climb – were not so bulky as to impede reserves moving around their reverse slopes to reinforce various parts of the line. The nature of the terrain meant that the Ethiopians could not encircle Baratieri's force, nor go around it unexpectedly and cut the Italian lines of communication. They would have had to charge directly against the Italian units, across ground favouring the defender.

Major-General Matteo Albertone was made second-in-command over Italian forces in Africa on 1 October 1889. Despite his many victories and long experience in the region, his misinterpretation of his movement order while in command of the Native Bde and the left column at Adowa was a major cause of the Italian defeat; it completely distorted the battle line on which Baratieri had intended to fight. Albertone was captured by the Ethiopians, and not released until 6 May 1897. (Courtesy SME/US)

THE BATTLE

The attacks on Albertone's command

It was Ras Alula's scouts who sighted Albertone's troops as they came into position; despite being on the Ethiopian left (north) wing, and thus furthest from Albertone's brigade, the victor of Dogali was the first to spot them because he had scouts active across the entire area. Soon the entire Ethiopian camp was alerted, and began forming up to envelop the invaders. On the right, south of Adowa, was King Tecla Aimanot and his troops from Gojjam, with the cavalry in front. In Adowa itself was Ras Mekonnen with his Harari troops. To the north of Adowa was Ras Mikael leading the Wollo Oromo. North of him was Ras Mangasha and his Tigré troops, and in the far north of the line was Ras Alula. In reserve on

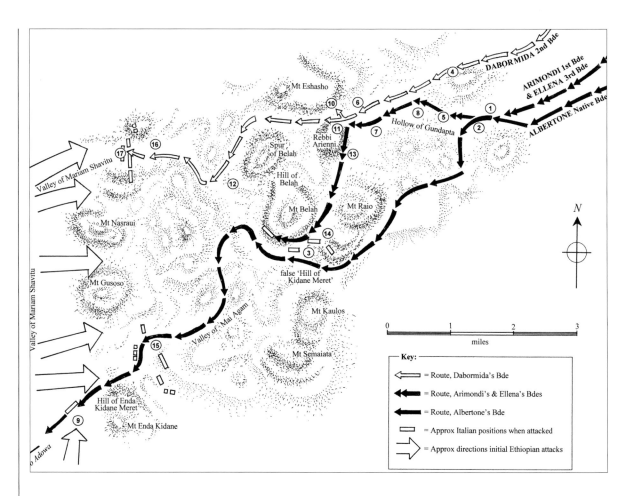

Italian deployments in the battle of Adowa, 1 March 1896

All timings are, inevitably, approximate:

(1) 3.30am: Head of Arimondi's 1st Bde reaches this point, to find path blocked by Albertone's Native Bde straying from their path just to the south. Arimondi held up for almost an hour as Albertone's troops pass.

(2) Albertone's troops swing south, back onto their designated path.

(3) 4am–4.30am: head of Albertone's Bde arrives at hill Baratieri calls 'Kidane Meret'; rear of column arrives at c.5am.

(4) c.4.50am: Head of Dabormida's 2nd Bde reaches this point.

(5) 4.30am: Head of Arimondi's Bde reaches this point.

(6) 6am: Dabormida deploys on Rebbi Arienni and southern slope of Mt Eshasho, remaining there until 6.45am.

(7) By 6.45am Arimondi's Bde is massed behind Dabormida.

(8) 6am: Maj De Amicis' 4th Inf Bn and company of Capt Pavesi's 5th Native Bn from Arimondi's Bde are ordered to this spot to secure Dabormida's line of retreat, but do not arrive until some time between 8.45am and 9.30am. At perhaps 10.30am they will be reinforced by Maj Rayneri's 13th Inf Bn from Dabormida's Bde.

(9) c.7.30am: Pushing ahead of Albertone's Bde, Maj Turitto's 1st Native Bn have reached this spot. They are fiercely engaged by Ethiopians, and withdraw, supported by De Luca's Hamacen irregulars.

(10) 6.30am–8.15am: Gen Baratieri is at Mt Eshasho.

(11) 6.30am–6.45am: When Dabormida returns from reconnoitring ahead, Baratieri orders him forward, to occupy the Spur of Belah. He orders Arimondi to occupy Rebbi Arienni, and Ellena to position his reserve on the western edge of Hollow of Gundapta.

(12) 6.45am: Asmara Kitet Co and part of Mobile Militia Bn from Dabormida's Bde advance on the Spur and Hill of Belah. They leave it at 7.45am, advancing behind left flank of Dabormida's column.

(13) 7.45am: Baratieri orders Arimondi to advance to a position opposite Mt Raio. At 8.15am he orders Ellena's reserve to occupy Rebbi Arienni.

(14) 9.12am: Baratieri and Arimondi arrive on a plateau of Mt Raio. Arimondi's troops deploy on the southern slopes of Mt Raio, the southern slope of the ridge between Mts Belah and Raio, and the western slopes of Mt Belah; all units are in place by 9.30am.

About an hour later the unguarded Spur of Belah is occupied by Ethiopians (see 12 above). Two companies of 2nd Bersaglieri Bn and units from Ellena's reserve try to retake it, but are repulsed with heavy losses. The Ethiopians then drive the 1st Bersaglieri Bn off the western slopes of Mt Belah, and break through the Italian centre.

(15) 8.15am: Albertone deploys here.

(16) 8.30am: Head of Dabormida's Bde is at this point, but his column stretches back all the way to Mt Eshasho.

(17) 9.30am: Dabormida deploys here.

the hills just west of Adowa, where the church of St George stands, were the Emperor Menelik and Empress Taitu, with the warriors of Ras Olié and Wagshum Guangul. The Oromo cavalry were grazing their ponies in meadows some 8 miles away, but they were soon informed of the situation, and mounted up. Menelik and Taitu went into the church of St George to pray; the empress, surrounded by her retainers, bent low with a stone on her neck, a traditional method of prayer in times of emergency. Nearby, priests from Axum carrying the Ark of the Covenant prayed for victory.

The Ethiopian units closest to Albertone's advanced position on the slopes of the Hill of Enda Kidane Meret first moved to the attack at perhaps 6am. These included troops under Menelik, King Tecla Aimanot, Ras Mikael, and Ras Mangasha, while those of Ras Mekonnen and Ras Olié came up soon after, so a large proportion of the Ethiopian army was soon concentrated against Albertone's isolated Native Brigade. The first of his units to come under fire was the 1st Native Bn, which itself had strayed too far ahead of Albertone's main body .

Still unaware of the dangerous position into which Albertone had got his brigade, Gen Baratieri spent a full hour going over the ground on which he planned to fight and preparing for an Ethiopian advance. He could hear firing in the distance, but assumed that it was only some pickets skirmishing. At 6.45am Baratieri gave another order that was wrongly interpreted. He told Dabormida to advance from Rebbi Arienni to the Spur of Belah to support by fire Albertone, whom he assumed to be at the 'false Kidane Meret' or at most a little ahead of it. However, once Dabormida got his 2nd Bde to a point west of the Spur, and discovered that Albertone was much further off than supposed, he continued to advance westwards – very slowly, across difficult ground. The nature of the terrain also led Dabormida further to the Italian right, so that – despite his mission to support Albertone – he in fact ended up in the west–east arm of the Mariam Shavitu valley, roughly in line with but about 3 miles north of the Native Brigade. The Spur of Belah was left unguarded after 7.45am (and a glance at the map will show how important it was to the Italian line). To add to the difficulties, Arimondi's 1st Bde had been stuck behind Dabormida on a single path while approaching Rebbi Arienni, so he was late getting all his men into position in the centre. The three

Major Turitto commanded the 1st Native Bn, the most advanced unit of Albertone's command at Adowa. (Piero Crociani Collection)

Ascari from Asmara. The African troops of Albertone's Native Bde had perhaps more training, and certainly more field experience, than the soldiers sent from Italy to reinforce the colony. They also tended to suffer much higher casualties, since they were often mutilated or killed if taken prisoner, so usually fought to the last. Note the Italian officer and African NCO standing behind the firing line – a practice that contributed to high casualties among junior leaders. (Piero Crociani Collection)

The view today looking south-west from Gen Ellena's position on Rabi Arienni. The Spur of Belah is to the right, and Mt Belah to the left, with the Hill of Belah between them. Most of Dabormida's Bde advanced westwards around the north of the Spur, off this photograph; only part of the Mobile Militia Bn and the Asmara Kitet Co occupied it briefly, via the Hill of Belah. (Author's photograph)

Taken from Baratieri's observation post on Mt Raio, looking north-west, with Mt Eshasho to the right. In the middleground, in the curve of the modern road, is Ellena's position on the lower hill of Rabi Arienni. Behind Rabi Arienni and left of Mt Eshasho is the route to the west taken by Dabormida's Brigade. (Author's photograph)

forward Italian brigades were now completely separated, and each would fight a more numerous foe, in three separate actions throughout the day. The Italian army had set itself up to be defeated in detail.

At 8.15am the morning mists cleared, and Gen Baratieri climbed part way up Mt Eshasho to survey the situation. He could see that Albertone was engaged, and that none of the other units was close enough to support him. But for some inexplicable reason, an hour later Dabormida reported that he was 'holding out his hand to Albertone'; this extraordinarily imprecise wording allowed Baratieri to assume that Dabormida was, at least, about to link up with Albertone – but this was not the case, and never would be. Baratieri headed south to another observation position on a plateau south of Mt Raio. This towering peak could only be climbed part way; as the author can confirm, the highest reachable ledge affords sweeping views in some directions, but not towards Albertone's positions.

Albertone's advanced 1st Native Bn saw tough fighting from about 7.30am to 8.30am, while the rest of the brigade were held back on hills north-east of Enda Kidane. Albertone's artillery inflicted heavy losses, but as the 1st Native Bn withdrew the Ethiopians rushed forward, destroyed the rearguard company, and drove the rest before them in panic flight. Albertone's main body managed to stop the Ethiopians once they came into rifle range, but by that time perhaps 18,000 warriors had begun to envelop the entire brigade with a half-moon formation. The stronger Ethiopian left (north) wing occupied Mt Gusoso between Albertone's and Dabormida's positions; this wing included men from the commands of Ras Mekonnen, Ras Mangasha, Ras Olié and Wagshum Guangul.

For a time the Italians held firm, inflicting heavy casualties, but then the Ethiopians set up 'quick-firing batteries' on Mt Enda Kidane, and Menelik committed thousands more warriors from his own command. Both flanks of the Native Bde soon collapsed, and at about 10.30am the badly mauled centre fell back to the north-east; the retreat soon turned into a rout, as Ethiopians rushed in on all sides. Two batteries tried to cover the withdrawal; one three-gun battery was captured, retaken by some ascari at bayonet-point, and then lost once more; the other batteries were also overrun, and their crews all but wiped out. General Albertone himself was captured. Locals still point out the spot where the fighting was hottest; they call it *Mindibdib*, 'cut to pieces'. Advancing bands of Ethiopian foot and horse soon filled the Mai Agam valley.

In the meantime, Baratieri had sent a message to Dabormida to help Albertone, but the messenger decided that he could turn back when he met the courier coming to inform Baratieri that Dabormida was 'holding out his hand' to Albertone. Baratieri sent two more messengers with the same order, but neither reached Dabormida. Baratieri still assumed that Dabormida had a solid hold on the Spur of Belah, covering Arimondi's right and the potential line of withdrawal. In fact Dabormida had sent only local auxiliaries to the Spur, and by about 9.30am they had been driven off it by infiltrating Ethiopians. Although Baratieri could not find Dabormida, the Ethiopians could; they had been attacking him fiercely since 9.30am, and had all but cut him off.

The centre and reserve

Baratieri organized Arimondi's command in the centre, reduced to 1,773 men because De Amicis' 4th Infantry Bn had been detached to cover Dabormida's potential line of retreat. The rest of Arimondi's men took up positions around Mt Belah and Mt Raio. Galliano's 3rd Native Bn from

Looking east from *Ras* Alula's viewpoint, up the west–east arm of the Mariam Shavitu valley towards Dabormida's final position, on hills to north and south and across the valley floor between them. For much of the day Dabormida's troops held their positions successfully, and even advanced; this was the site of heavy Ethiopian losses. (Author's photograph)

Major-General Vittorio Dabormida, killed while commanding the 2nd Infantry Bde and the right column at Adowa. Although he was given an ill-informed movement order by Gen Baratieri, his subsequent deployment, and his failures of communication, played a major part in the defeat. (Courtesy SME/US)

Gen Ellena's reserve was hurried forward and positioned on Arimondi's left wing. Ellena's two quick-firer batteries were also brought up, while the rest of his force remained at Rebbi Arienni.

By 10am Arimondi's men were opening fire on Ethiopians pursuing the fleeing remnants of Albertone's brigade north-eastwards up the Mai Agam valley; they had to pick their targets carefully, however, as the warriors kept close behind the Italians. Small groups of Ethiopians crouched low and worked their way into position to face this new enemy. As these warriors sniped at Arimondi's gun-crews and infantry, a large group of their countrymen appeared in the valley in front of the Spur of Belah, and poured up its slopes at about 10.30am. One wing – the same warriors who had driven a wedge between Albertone's right and Dabormida's left – swung around to their right to hit Ellena's reserve force. Dabormida's 2nd Bde, and De Amicis' battalion far behind it, were now completely cut off. Two companies of Bersaglieri from Arimondi's command and a regiment from Ellena's reserve tried to retake the Spur, but were annihilated.

The attack on Dabormida's command

Warriors under Ras Mikael and Ras Mangasha, and a detachment of Ras Mekonnen's men – some 15,000 warriors, with more coming – had spent the early morning mauling Albertone's force, but once the Native Bde was doomed to destruction they took on the newly arrived Italian infantry to its north.

Shortly after 9am, Dabormida's four advance companies had been attacked in overwhelming strength and beaten in 20 minutes. They were only a few hundred yards ahead of the main body of 2nd Bde, but invisible beyond a pair of steep ridges covered in thorn bushes. Soon the Ethiopians came upon Dabormida's main line; this was anchored to high hills on its north and south flanks and stretched across the west–east arm of the Mariam Shavitu valley. The ascari charged twice, pushing the Ethiopians back with bayonets; the warriors approached more carefully after that, creeping through the high grass covering most of this area and sniping as they came. Once they got in close, they leapt up and charged, supported by hundreds of Oromo cavalry, but orderly rifle volleys and accurate artillery fire repulsed this attack as well.

The firing became desultory; the Ethiopians seem to have been limiting themselves to a holding engagement in this sector, and at around noon Dabormida ordered an advance. His line of retreat was covered by De Amicis' 4th Infantry Bn and the native Kitet Company from Asmara under Capt Sermasi, who at 9.30am had positioned themselves on a small hill between the Spur and Dabormida's position in the Mariam Shavitu valley. During the next couple of hours Dabormida's troops stopped all Ethiopian attempts at envelopment; his artillery bombarded the Ethiopians and their cannons posted on the heights before him, but numerous charges by his infantry could not dislodge them. A final furious charge succeeded; but shortly thereafter – at about 1pm – a large body of Ethiopian infantry and cavalry with three guns swooped up from the south and put themselves between Dabormida's new advanced position and De Amicis, although they were quickly pushed back. At the same time other warriors attacked Dabormida's right flank.

While this evidence of enemy in his rear must have worried Dabormida, he did not know that his was now the only Italian force still

The view south-eastwards from Dabormida's position, across the Mai Agam valley between the two chains of mountains – note that the 'valley' is in fact very uneven and broken terrain. On the left is Mt Belah, and in the right distance Mt Kaulos. The plateau on the centre skyline is the 'false Kidane Meret', which Baratieri had intended should be occupied by Albertone's command. (Author's photograph)

intact. Albertone had been overwhelmed; the centre under Arimondi was threatened from both its left and right flanks; Ellena's reserve was engaged, and with Ethiopians now as far east as the Hollow of Gundapta the army's route of retreat was threatened. Lieutenant-Colonel Galliano's 3rd Native Bn, covering Arimondi's left, now broke and fled, the officers and a few ascari who remained with them soon being overwhelmed.

General Dabormida had been fighting mostly against Ras Alula's troops, but now the bulk of the Ethiopians – some 40,000 men – turned on 2nd Brigade. By 2pm Dabormida, still unaware of the rout of the rest of the army, was nearly surrounded. His men were exhausted by their night march and long day's fighting, suffering from thirst and hunger, and running low on ammunition. Dabormida ordered a final attack that temporarily pushed the Ethiopians back, allowing him to sound the retreat at perhaps 4.30pm. As with the Albertone, the Ethiopians came in close and harried the retreat from three sides. Two guns that tried to cover the retreat soon ran out of ammunition; they were overrun and their crews were killed to a man. The remnants of Dabormida's force only escaped after great loss.

Dabormida himself was killed by a warrior named Shaqa Tamre, whom the English traveller Augustus Wylde interviewed shortly after the battle: 'Dabormida had just shot three men with his revolver, he then shot at my informant and missed him. The Abyssinian got behind a tree, and when Dabormida turned to face another of his enemies he shot him dead… This man carried off the General's sword, photographs, pocket-book and some other property, and afterwards sold them to an Italian officer who was a prisoner at Adese Ababa [sic].'

Retreat and pursuit
General Baratieri, realizing that the battle was lost, ordered a general retreat. He tried to get the last uncommitted units of the reserve – 16th Native Bn, and two companies of the 5th Infantry Regt's Alpini battalion – to cover the retreat, but before they could form up their lines were broken by a flood of fleeing soldiers intermingled with Ethiopians. Soon this final reserve was taking fire at close range from every angle – even from above, because the Ethiopians had now taken Mt Belah. The reserve had no chance to form a coherent defence, and soon got swept along with the tide. The Italian centre was now completely broken. Arimondi's mule

ran away in the confusion, and the general was killed along with many of his men.

The retreat was ill-coordinated owing to the impossibility of getting orders to all parts of the broken line, but by noon the remainder of Albertone's, Arimondi's, and Ellena's troops were all withdrawing. A late arrival on the field, Capt Franzini's artillery battery, showed up in time to get off just one shot before being overrun. A few isolated groups of ascari and Italians managed to engage in a fighting retreat – forming lines, firing, retreating a short distance, then forming and firing again – but they were in the minority. There were many instances of heroism by individuals and small parties, but most of the Italian army had become a fleeing mob, firing only when an Ethiopian appeared from behind a rock or tree to take a shot from point-blank range. Any Italian or ascaro who fell wounded was dispatched with spear or sword, and only a few managed to surrender alive; whether or not they could be considered lucky depended on their later fate. (There were reports of some officers and men shooting themselves to avoid capture.) In his memoirs, Gen Baratieri describes the disintegration of his army:

> *The firing continued from the heights, on the flanks, and in the rear; and already, the ranks being broken, the tail of the retiring column became a confused mass of white men and black men, Ascari of Galliano, and Ascari of the other units, together with the Shoans [enemy], who dashed into the middle of them… Every moment the confusion kept increasing owing to the waves of men sweeping by, the hail of bullets, and the sight of the dead and dying… while one's heart was being torn in two by the despair of ever being able to give an order or get it carried out.*

Baratieri reached Rebbi Arienni, where he managed to rally about a hundred Bersaglieri and Alpini. The Italians managed to push back the first wave of pursuers at the point of the bayonet, but the Ethiopian numbers soon swelled, and once again Baratieri had to retreat. Together with Gen Ellena he remained at the rear of the retreating column, trying in vain to organize a rearguard action. Baratieri recalls the state of his men at this time:

> *They were almost unconscious of their surroundings, and careless of everything except their personal defence. The officers had lost authority over the soldiers, who looked in a bewildered and stupefied manner at those who gave an order or attempted to halt them.*

The Oromo cavalry swooped in on the weary, thirsty fugitives, riding up close to empty pistols into their ranks. More and more men got left behind; a few isolated pockets, completely surrounded, continued to resist, and firing could be heard on Mt Raio until 4pm. All of these remnants of the Italian army were wiped out or captured.

The main column under Baratieri, which was retreating northwards, was harried for 9 miles before the Ethiopian warriors gave up the pursuit, but beacon fires were then lit on the highest hilltops to signal the people of the countryside to rise and attack. The numbers can never be known, but it is certain that many Italian and ascari stragglers fell victim to vengeful peasants. Baratieri's shattered army continued to retreat through the night of 1/2 March. The vanguard with the guides became separated from the main body in the darkness, and the troops under Gen Baratieri got lost three times. The main groups of survivors crossed the Belesa river and reached Adi Caieh and Adi Ugri – some 40 miles north of Adowa – on 3 and 4 March.

Back at the battlefield the Ethiopians were celebrating. They chanted 'Mow, mow down the tender grass! The corn of Italy that was sown in Tigré has been reaped by Menelik, and he has given it to the birds!'

Contemporary Italian artist's impression of the last stand of Dabormida's Brigade. The artist has put the Ethiopians far too close to a still-formed Italian line; by the time they got within this range Menelik's warriors would be charging with swords drawn, at broken remnants. (Courtesy Prof Luigi Goglia, Director, Laboratorio di ricerca e documentazione storica iconografica, Facoltà di Scienze- Poliche, Università Roma – hereafter, LRDSI/UR)

The cost, and the aftermath

On the battlefield and during the retreat the Italians lost a total of 6,133 men killed: 261 officers, 2,918 white NCOs and privates, 954 permanently missing, and about 2,000 ascari. Another 1,428 were wounded – 470 Italians (including 31 officers) and 958 ascari. The Ethiopians captured all 56 Italian guns. This was by far the most costly defeat yet suffered by a white colonial force at the hands of non-European enemies.[1] Although absolute accuracy is impossible, the total casualties represented about 53 per cent of Gen Baratieri's command. Ethiopian losses are unclear, but are estimated to have been about 7,000 killed and 10,000 wounded – huge numbers, but still a far smaller percentage of their total strength in the field.

The Ethiopians took about 3,000–4,000 prisoners. Ascari who had been recruited in Tigré itself were considered to be traitors, and an estimated 800 of them had their right hand and left foot cut off; some were castrated. Despite individual horror stories, the Italians were generally treated better, but many died in the harsh conditions of the marches and camps they had to endure before their release, which began in May 1896.

This disastrous defeat had immediate repercussions in Italy. Prime Minister Crispi's bellicose government fell. Baratieri was stripped of his governorship and court-martialed, the official reason being that he had abandoned his troops. He was rightly acquitted of this charge, but the tribunal declared him 'entirely unfitted to cope with the exigencies of the situation', and he retired in disgrace. The new government in Rome at once authorized his replacement, Gen Baldissera, to sue for peace. Menelik was already scouting out the road to Asmara when the envoy Maj Salsa brought him Rome's offer of peace. Menelik agreed not to cross the Mereb river into the colony, in return for the immediate removal of the Italian troops at Adigrat; Salsa agreed, and promised more detailed discussions in the near future. In the event, Italian colonial expansion in Eritrea was abandoned for about 15 years.

---

1 The British defeat by the Zulus at Isandlwana in January 1879 had cost Chelmsford about 1,360 men, perhaps 800 of them British regulars. General Baratieri's dubious record would stand until July–August 1921, when Gen Silvestre's Spanish army in north-east Morocco lost some 13,200 men killed by Rif Berbers at Anual and during the subsequent retreat.

Two Italian survivors of Adowa after their return to Massawa. Stragglers limped into Italian Eritrea for weeks after the battle, exhausted, barefoot, and with their uniforms in rags. (Courtesy SME/US)

Historians have debated why Menelik did not follow up his victory. Ras Alula complained, 'I asked the king to give me his cavalry… and if he had, I would have driven the Italians into the sea.' Several reasons present themselves. Firstly, Menelik knew that Eritrea was still heavily garrisoned, with 16,700 troops guarding well-fortified positions; he had humiliated Italian arms, but if he pressed forward this garrison might be reinforced. Secondly, he was short of provisions; Eritrea was suffering a famine, and the region lay beyond his line of food depots. Thirdly, he wanted to consolidate his authority over the western, eastern, and southern peripheries of his kingdom. These territories were as rich as Eritrea, and easier to conquer; if he did not take them, then the British and Egyptians, the Mahdists, or the French – eager for a foothold in the Upper Sudan – might get them first. Fourthly, in Eritrea he would be reconquering populations once ruled by, and still loyal to, his former rival for the throne, Ras Mangasha. Finally, he was worried that if he entered lands that he had formally ceded under the Treaty of Wuchale, the European powers might cast him as the aggressor, and support Italy.

As it turned out, Menelik II earned more than a name for himself in the annals of military history; he earned a place in the family of nations. The Treaty of Addis Ababa, signed with Italy on 26 October 1896, recognized Ethiopian sovereignty and repealed Article 17 of the Treaty of Wuchale. In return, Menelik recognized Eritrea as an Italian colony. Unlike the earlier agreement, it was not written in Amharic and Italian, but in Amharic and French, in order to avoid any deliberate 'misunderstandings'. The European powers met with Menelik, and defined his country's boundaries in relation to their own colonies. Menelik hired European technicians to build infrastructure such as roads and telegraph lines – as well as Ethiopia's first railway, leading from Addis Ababa to the French port of Obok (Djibouti). This more than compensated for the loss of Massawa.

The decisive victory at Adowa led to a European reappraisal of the Ethiopians. They had proved capable of mobilizing a large army for a sustained campaign, and defeating a sizeable European force. The public dealt with this challenge to European racial assumptions in various ways. Some blamed bad Italian soldiering, while others changed their view of the Ethiopians. Before Adowa, the European media referred to the Ethiopians as black Africans; after Adowa, they called them bronze Semites. Menelik himself approved of this concept. When later asked to lead a Pan African Council, he replied that it was 'an excellent idea… The Negro should be uplifted… I wish you the greatest possible success. But in coming to me to take the leadership, you are knocking at the wrong door, so to speak. You know, I am not a Negro at all. I am a Caucasian.'

THE ETHIOPIAN ARMY

Like many tribal societies, the ethnic groups of Ethiopia put a strong emphasis on martial ability. Boys were trained from early childhood in the use of the sword, spear and shield. Every man yearned to own a gun, not just for what it would do for him on the battlefield, but also for hunting. The character of Ethiopian fighting men can hardly be summed

(continued on page 33)

ETHIOPIAN LEADERS
1: *Negus Negasti* Menelik II
2: *Ras* Mekonnen

A

ETHIOPIAN WARRIORS
1: Infantry swordsman
2: Infantry officer, Tigré
3: Amhara rifleman, Shewa

B

SUDANESE MAHDIST WARRIORS
1: Baqqara cavalryman
2: Sudanese footsoldier

1

2

ITALIAN INFANTRY, 1895–96
1 & 2: Private, *Cacciatori d'Africa*, marching order
3: Corporal, *Fanteria d'Africa*, marching order

D

CAVALRY
1: Ethiopian Oromo horseman
2: Ascari, native cavalry *'Penne di Falco'*; Kassala, 1894

E

ITALIAN OFFICERS, 1895–96
1: Artillery lieutenant, marching order
2: Beni Amer guide
3: Captain, *Fanteria d'Africa*, marching order
4: Captain, *Cacciatori d'Africa*, full dress

1

2

3

4

F

ASCARI, 1895–96
1: Habab irregular
2: *Ascaro*, 2nd Eritrean Bn 'Hidalgo'
3: *Sciumbasi*, 6th Eritrean Bn 'Cossu'

1

2

3

G

ITALIAN OFFICERS & NCO, 1895–96
1: Sergeant-major, *Fanteria d'Africa*, marching order
2: Infantry captain, *Truppe d'Africa*, service dress
3: Lieutenant, *Bersaglieri*,
   marching order

1

2

3

H

up better than by this passage from one of the bardic songs sung by their *azmari* praise-singers, in this case to rally wavering warriors:

Brothers, are ye hungry? Are ye
thirsty?
Oh true sons of my mother, are ye
not birds of prey?
Forward! Behold the flesh of your
enemy,
And I will be the carver of your
feast!
Forward! If ye lack honey-wine,
I will give you blood to drink!

The Italians faced an Ethiopian army larger and more organized than in all of its recent history. Menelik had centralized and streamlined the taxation system, bringing in more goods to the central government. This allowed Menelik to keep a larger standing army, and support a huge temporary army at need. Most taxes were in kind – food or labour that went directly to support the soldiers. Menelik also ordered an extensive geographical survey in order to increase revenue, and to identify land that could be given to soldiers as a reward. His government also enjoyed the revenue from customs duties on ever-increasing international trade.

Mobilization and logistics

While the emperor maintained only a relatively small standing army, the entire countryside could be mobilized when a Negus ordered a *kitet*, or call to arms. This was made by proclamations in marketplaces and other gathering spots, and large *negarit* war drums were beaten to alert outlying farms. One even acted as a platform for the messenger, who stood on an upturned drum and read the proclamation while a slave held his lance and robe next to him as symbols of his rank. While the king was not always in full control of his territory, 'beating the *kitet*' was generally effective; it usually summoned men to fight against a common enemy, and always offered a chance for plunder and prestige.

The Ethiopian army on the march looked more like a migration. Many warriors brought their families along, and wives and children would cook and gather provisions and firewood. During the march there were no stops until a camp was found for the night. The wealthier warriors had servants to carry their equipment and mules or horses to ride. All these extra people and animals had to be fed, increasing the need to keep mobile. While some food was carried by the men themselves or on muleback, the army was expected to live off the land, and foragers spread out over a large area. The central highlands of Ethiopia are green and filled with game, so as long as an army kept moving it could feed itself, and, being relatively unburdened, it could move quickly. If it stopped for long, however, it would soon starve; this was a major problem if the army had to besiege a fortification, or – as in the run-up to Adowa – wait for an enemy to make the first move. Menelik realized that the large force he

Italian and *ascari* prisoners shortly after their release, probably in May 1896. The *ascari* recruited in the northern provinces of Tigré had their right hand and left foot cut off by their Ethiopian captors as punishment for treason – see left foreground. Italian prisoners were occasionally mistreated, but most of those who died in captivity succumbed to untreated wounds, sickness, or exhaustion during the hard marches of the Ethiopian army. (Courtesy Prof Luigi Goglia, LRDSI/UR)

Le Petit Journal

SUPPLÉMENT ILLUSTRÉ

DIMANCHE 28 AOUT 1898

Le Nègus Ménélik à la bataille d'Adoua

Menelik captured the European imagination by his victory over the Italians; the London *Times* wrote that 'This victory will arouse the spirit of Africans who until today have been treated with contempt... [Menelik's] victory is the victory of all Africa.' The cover of this Paris weekly magazine printed in August 1898 shows a surprisingly accurate image of the Ethiopian army on the march. (Bertrand Duqénois Collection, www.dear-ethiopia.com)

was assembling might run into difficulties of supply, especially considering that some regions he planned to march through were suffering from famine, so he ordered depots of food to be placed at regular intervals along the lines of march. This allowed Menelik to wait out the Italians on a couple of occasions.

This need for strategic speed affected how the Ethiopians made war. They avoided long conflicts in favour of big showdown battles in which they could destroy the enemy army and force favourable terms from the enemy commander. Drawn-out campaigns could prove counter-productive, since the army would have to ravage the very land they sought to conquer, forcing the inhabitants to flee. During Menelik's long wait before Adowa the area was picked clean of food and most of the trees were chopped down for firewood. Shortages of ammunition, and the often fragile coalitions among the leaders, also encouraged quick campaigns.

To aid the advance, teams of workmen moved ahead of the main army clearing the way of trees and stones and searching out the best passes through the mountains. The Negus Negasti kept a group that outsiders called the 'Royal Engineers', but while some were undoubtedly skilled at complex operations such as building bridges, most were simply labourers.

Tactics

Ethiopians favoured a half-moon formation in order to outflank and envelop an enemy, although extreme terrain often made this impossible. Despite having a general plan, warriors fought more or less as individuals, advancing and retreating as they saw fit. Chiefs only had a loose control over their men, and never kept them in close formation except for the final charge, when everyone bunched together and hurried to be the first to reach the foe. Considering the lethal effectiveness of late 19th-century rifles, this loose mode of fighting was actually in advance of its day. The Ethiopian tendency was to get in close to ensure a good shot, although rushing *en masse* when the enemy appeared weak did lead to great losses. The Italian army, especially the ascari, showed good discipline under fire, and inflicted heavy casualties on the Ethiopians; the majority of these tended to be suffered during the final rush. When charging, the Ethiopians used various battle cries depending on their origin: the Oromo shouted 'Slay! Slay!', while warriors from Gojjam cried 'God pardon us, Christ!', and those from Shewa rallied to the call 'Together! Together!'

The Ethiopians had no formal medical corps. Healers trained in traditional medicine followed the army, but were too few to care adequately for the huge numbers of casualties. Still, traditional healers did the best they could at setting limbs and cleaning out wounds. One method for sanitizing gunshot wounds was to pour melted butter mixed with the local herb *fetho* (lapidum sativum) into the wound. In battle the warriors' families cared for the wounded, collected guns from the fallen to distribute to poorly armed warriors, and fetched water for those fighting. This last detail was important; at Adowa, Itegue Taitu had at least

10,000 women bringing water to the warriors, while the Italians suffered from thirst throughout the day.

The Ethiopians lacked uniforms; common warriors wore their everyday clothing – generally a white, cream, or brown length of cotton called a *shamma* that was wound around the body in various ways. Chiefs and higher nobility wore a variety of colourful garments, including the *lembd*, a ceremonial item vaguely resembling the cope or dalmatic of Christian churchmen (see 'Plate Commentaries', below). If a man had slain a lion during his career, his formal clothing could be embellished with the lion's mane.

Rifles

Despite Western preconceptions, and the employment of antique firearms by the poorest warriors, the majority of Ethiopians were armed with large-calibre, breech-loading, mostly single-shot rifles no more than 30 years old since they had first appeared in Western armies. It is estimated that Menelik's army may have had as many as 100,000 of such weapons in 1896. Until the collapse of diplomatic relations he had been able to purchase large numbers of rifles from the Italians, and also from the Russians, French and British. After Italian sources dried up Menelik strove to increase his other imports, and a key figure in this trade was Ras Mekonnen of Harar, a city in eastern Ethiopia with trade links to the Red Sea. Individual chiefs also stockpiled arms, and issued them to their best warriors in times of need.

The types used by the Ethiopians included the elderly British 1866/67 Snider – an 1856 Enfield muzzle-loader converted into a single-shot breech-loader. Used on the British Magdala expedition of 1867–68 against the Emperor Tewodros II, it had a massive 14.6mm calibre and a hinged breech action. However, the Ethiopians also had considerable numbers of the superior 1871 Martini-Henry – the classic British single-shot, lever-action, falling-block weapon of the colonial wars, firing 11.43mm bullets.

The French 1866 Chassepot was another second-generation breech-loader, a bolt-action, single-shot weapon taking 11mm paper and card cartridges; but again, the Ethiopians also had larger numbers of more modern 1871 Le Gras rifles, in which the Chassepot's paper cartridges were replaced with 11mm brass rounds. Menelik's warriors even had some 1886 Lebel 8mm bolt-action magazine rifles; with eight cartridges in the tubular magazine below the barrel, one in the cradle behind the chamber and one 'up the spout', these took ten rounds. The Lebel's smaller-bore, smokeless-powder ammunition was the most advanced in the world (all the other types took black-powder rounds, which produced a giveaway cloud of white smoke and fouled the chamber fairly quickly with continuous firing).

The Peabody-Martini was an 1870 Swiss modification of an 1862 Peabody design from the United States. Widely manufactured across Europe, it had a single-shot, falling-block action in various calibres from 10.41mm to 11.43 mm. Probably the single most common rifle in Ethiopian use was the 'rolling-block' Remington, another American design very widely built

This Ethiopian chief rides a horse with highly decorated trappings, probably of brass or silver. His follower carries a traditional round shield with added decoration of brass or silver, and a Vetterli M1870/87 rifle. This photo was taken in 1890, so the rifle was probably legally purchased from Italy in the days before the arms embargo. The Ethiopians were amazed at how easy it was to buy guns from the Europeans, as expressed in a poem from the period:
'What a fool he is, the person from a European country; How, having made the instrument of death, can he give it away? With the Vetterli that he bought, with the bullets that he bought, Menelik roasted and cracked the foreign barley.'
(Courtesy SME/US)

under licence in the 1860s–80s, in calibres up to 12.7mm (.50 calibre). The Winchester 1866 was a lever-action 11.18mm calibre weapon with a tubular magazine taking 12 rounds; several later models used a box magazine. The Russians had supplied the Ethiopians with a fair number of US-designed, Russian-made Berdan 1864 and 1870 rifles; both were single-shot 10.75mm weapons, the 1864 model with a hinged 'trapdoor' breech and the 1870 with a bolt action. Sources also mention German Mausers, most likely the 11mm single-shot, bolt-action 1871 model. The Ethiopians also had some examples of the Austrian 1878 Kropatschek, an 11mm bolt-action repeater with an eight-round tubular magazine.

This wide variety of rifles and calibres inevitably created local shortages of ammunition. Menelik instituted a quartermaster system, and individual leaders may have helped supply individuals who were short of cartridges, but in general each man was expected to supply his own (and probably 'collected his brass' for artisan reloading). Cartridges were so valuable they were often used as currency; being hoarded, they tended to be older than was ideal, but Menelik and other leaders strove to purchase as much new ammunition as possible, and it appears that his forces at Adowa were well supplied. Still, out of habit the Ethiopian soldier conserved his ammunition, preferring to get up close before firing. Wylde noted they 'made good practice at up to about 400–600 yards, and at a short distance they are as good shots as any men in Africa, the Transvaal Boers not excepted, as they never throw away a cartridge if they can help it and never shoot in a hurry'.

Traditional weapons

Despite the wide availability of firearms, many Ethiopians still went into battle with more traditional weapons. The *shotel* was the favoured type of sword, a heavy steel weapon curved like a scimitar, but with the sharpened edge usually on the inside of the curve so that the warrior could stab around the edge of an opponent's shield. It was carried slung on the right side, so that the left (shield) arm had a full range of movement. Steel-headed spears were pretty much universal among men and boys for defending their flocks from wild animals; generally about 6ft long with a leaf-shaped head, they could be thrown, but were more often used for thrusting. Small shields completed an Ethiopian warrior's kit. Styles varied among the tribes, but the most common was a circular, conical shield made of hide and covered on the front with coloured cloth such as velvet. Many were decorated and strengthened with strips of brass, tin or more valuable metals; a shield was an easy way for a warrior to show off his wealth and status, and many were quite elaborate.

Cavalry was common in the Ethiopian lowlands, and the horsemen of the Oromo were especially renowned. Horses were useful and acted as a

An Ethiopian warrior armed with a typical wide-bladed thrusting spear; his shield is a nearly flat circle of undecorated animal hide, indicating that he is of low status and wealth. He wears a *shamma*, the robe worn to this day in the Ethiopian countryside. It can be wound around the body in a number of ways, but for battle the right arm would always be left free. (Courtesy SME/US)

The French Le Gras M1871 rifle was popular with the Ethiopians, and large numbers of them were imported secretly – many through the town of Harar, where the French poet Arthur Rimbaud worked as an arms dealer.
The 11mm Gras was typical of the fairly modern generation of weapons acquired by the Ethiopians; even after the introduction of the revolutionary M1886 Lebel, it had remained standard French Army issue in their colonies until c.1892–95. (Piero Crociani Collection)

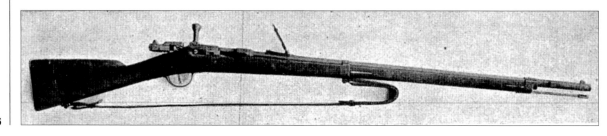

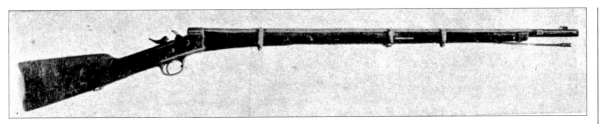

status symbol, so every warrior wanted one. The Ethiopian horse is smaller than its European counterpart and can negotiate terrain that would stop a European steed. Nevertheless, Ethiopia's mountainous terrain and dense thickets of thorn-bushes often meant that battles had to be fought on foot. Weaponry for cavalrymen was identical to that for footsoldiers.

Artillery

The Ethiopians had 42 guns at Adowa. It is unclear what types of cannon were used, but sources agree that they were a mix of older guns bought or captured from various sources. They included Krupps, and mountain guns captured from the Egyptians when they tried to take Ethiopian territory in 1875 and 1876, or left behind when the Egyptian garrison evacuated Harar in 1885. One source describes the artillery as 'of all calibres and systems'. There was a chronic shortage of shells, and thus crews had little chance to practise. While the Ethiopians were capable of bombarding a fort, as at Mekele, they had difficulty in manoeuvring guns and laying down accurate fire in broken terrain against a moving enemy; Italian eyewitnesses said that the Ethiopian artillery made a poor performance at Adowa.

More effective were the several automatic cannon that Menelik brought to Adowa. A detailed listing is unavailable, but Maxim weapons are mentioned, and perhaps six were 37mm Hotchkiss pieces. Produced by an American company from 1875, these were later licence-built in Europe, particularly France. Early versions were multi-barrel revolvers, fired by turning a crank like a Gatling gun; later models had a single barrel and were fed by a belt. These later-model 'pom-poms' fired both solid and explosive rounds, and were superior in range and accuracy to the Italian artillery.

Remington 'rolling-block' rifles of various calibres were used by both sides in 1896; the Ethiopians had them in great numbers, and they were deliberately issued to some Italian reinforcements in 1895/96 in place of the latest 6.5mm M1891 Carcano. Reportedly, men trained on bolt-action rifles found the Remington action awkward to master; even though it is simple enough, it certainly limited the rate of fire. (Piero Crociani Collection)

An *ascaro* photographed in 1896 armed with a Sudanese *kaskara* sword. The *ascari* often replaced worn-out items of Italian kit with those of African manufacture. Note the red chevron of a *muntaz* on his upper sleeves. (Courtesy SME/US)

The Ethiopian Army at Adowa, 1 March 1896

Negus Negasti Menelik: 25,000 rifles, 3,000 horses, 32 guns
Itegue Taitu: 3,000 rifles, 600 horses, 4 guns
Negus Tecla Aimanot: 5,000 rifles
Ras Mekonnen: 15,000 rifles
Ras Mangasha and Ras Alula: 12,000 rifles, 6 guns
Ras Mangasha Atichim: 6,000 rifles
Ras Mikael: 6,000 rifles, 5,000 horses
Ras Oliè and others: 8,000 rifles
Totals: 80,000 rifles, 8,600 horses, 42 guns

Note: These are the figures given by two observers, Lt Melli and the Russian traveller Elez. Additionally there were about 20,000 spearmen and swordsmen, mostly on foot, and an unknown number of armed peasants – some Tigré locals, some rebels from Eritrea. Other writers believe that total Ethiopian strength was as high as 120,000 men. Given the nature of the Ethiopian army, the commanders themselves would not have known the precise numbers of warriors under their command. In addition to these figures, thousands of camp followers added 25–35 per cent to the total.

THE ITALIAN ARMY

Character and composition

Most of the colonial army that faced this exotic but highly effective force was made up of Eritrean or Sudanese troops – ascari. While some of the Italian officers and soldiers of the Corpo Speciale d'Africa had been in the colony for months or even years, most of the formed Italian units were new arrivals with only a vague idea of where they were or what they faced. The garrison troops were supplemented by hired Eritrean irregulars, who were little different from the warriors who fought under Menelik.

The Italian Army was raised by conscription, for three years' service with the colours followed by a reserve obligation. Service was generally regarded as a rite of manhood and 'school of the nation'; however, even on home service the efficiency and internal cohesion of most regiments were hampered by Italy's chronic localism. The government's obsession with unifying the Italian population led to an unwieldy system of posting units away from their recruitment areas, and mixing sub-units from different regions (and thus speaking different dialects). The mutual incomprehension between officers speaking Tuscan Italian and the bulk of their illiterate rankers widened an already yawning social gulf.

Late 19th-century European observers generally had a low opinion of the Italian Army. Italian generals and their troops had performed badly against the Austrians in 1866 (when Italy had tried to snatch a profit from the brief Austro-Prussian War), and their victories against the poorly-armed and disorganized Mahdists were considered insufficient proof of their ability. It must be remembered, however, that at Adowa the Italians and ascari fought stubbornly against a vastly superior force of Ethiopians for most of the day. Ethiopian eyewitnesses, even in the midst of exulting over their victory, made note that the Italian side fought bravely; and all sources agree that the ascari were as good as – or better than – the Italian regulars.

While the more experienced Italian colonial troops and ascari acquitted themselves well, the most recent arrivals from Italy were less reliable. The units were raised from individual conscripts who volunteered for African service, formed into new battalions numbered in sequence, which were organized into purely tactical regiments and brigades. Sources for the renumbering are confusing, but it appears that only the 1st, 2nd and 3rd Bns of *Fanteria d'Africa* had served in Africa prior to December 1895, and that the higher-numbered battalions were sent to the front almost straight from the harbour.

Italian NCOS and officers posing at Mekele in 1895, uniformed in differing shades of khaki and in white; three in the foreground wear the dark blue cap illustrated in Plate H1. They come from a variety of branches – crossed cannons are just visible on the cap of the artillery NCO reclining on the right. (Courtesy SME/US)

Unfamiliar with the country and climate, they naturally suffered from the hot days, cold nights, strange food and unforgiving terrain. This ignorance was shared by both officers and men, who had been thrown together with little time to get to know each other. This inevitably led to confusion both in camp and in the field, and one witness states that when asked what unit they were in, many newcomers replied with the number of their old unit back home. Some officers only found out which troops they were to command at the last moment, and simply wrote their branch, battalion and regiment in ink on their sun helmets.

An African NCO overseeing practice with a Gardner machine gun in Eritrea. Automatic weapons, so effective in the British campaigns in the Sudan, were not used to any great extent by the Italians. Due to imprecise terminology, the documentary record is unclear as to how many there were in the colony, or if any were used at Adowa. If they were, they played no significant part in the battle. (Courtesy SME/US)

While the original, genuine volunteers for colonial service were presumably eager, those shipped out in 1895–96 had been gathered with a degree of compulsion, and it is also highly questionable how much useful training they had received before Adowa. The rapidly dwindling morale of these newcomers was one factor in Gen Baratieri's decision to advance on 29 February 1896. Fresh from Italy, with racist assumptions about how easy it would be to defeat the Ethiopians, the new arrivals started grumbling while the army waited at Sauria, and morale and discipline withered. The ascari were apparently unimpressed by what they saw of the Italian rank and file.

The Italian battalions had 450–500 rifles each (see order of battle). The native battalions had been much larger, consisting of five companies of 250 men; after the middle of 1895 this changed to four companies of 300 men each, but the battalions' field strength at Adowa was usually below 1,000 rifles. Companies were divided into 'centurias' of 100 men, and these into 'buluks' of 25 men. An Italian major commanded each battalion, and an Italian captain each company, assisted by two Italian lieutenants and an Italian NCO; after the 1895 reform a third Italian lieutenant was added. Natives were not eligible for these positions, but could rise to the rank of *jus-bashi* (subaltern), of which there were two per company. Originally the company had included Italian sergeants, but these men resented taking orders from their native superiors and their employment was soon discontinued.

Logistics

The equipment provided for Italian units was often substandard. For example, the heavy boots were unsuited for the terrain, caused no end of pain for the average soldier, and also wore out quickly. General Baratieri had repeatedly requested proper alpine boots, but never received them. Near the end of the battle of Adowa, Italian soldiers were seen taking boots off their dead comrades to replace their own worn-out

Bersaglieri ready to go out on manoeuvres from Saati in 1888. The rarity of photos of Italian infantry in the 1896 campaign is due to the fact that most of the correspondents in Eritrea, foreseeing that the expedition would end badly, chose to remain in Massawa; the only photographer to accompany the advance, Pippo Ledru, lost his equipment at Adowa. Note the two mules with water kegs; water was a constant problem for the Italians, as the local water often made them sick, and the highlands can be very dry. (Courtesy SME/US)

One of the dozens of brass Type 75B mountain guns captured by the Ethiopians at Adowa, later recaptured during the Italian invasion of 1935–36; several are now on display at the Museo Storico della Fanteria in Rome. In rough terrain these weapons could be disassembled easily into loads for mules, or even for teams of men. (Author's photograph)

ones. The uniforms were too hot for the climate, and got torn to shreds by thorn-bushes. Tools such as picks and shovels were of inferior quality and soon wore out in use on the rocky soil, and even many bayonets and rifles had become unusable by the time they were needed at Adowa.

There were also gaps in the Italians' logistics. The food supply was unreliable, and the men often had to subsist on half rations; much of the fatigue that the soldiers showed in the later hours of the battle of Adowa may be attributed to this. The fact that the available rations were expected to give out on 2 or 3 March was one of the reasons that Baratieri gave for advancing against Menelik on 29 February. There was also a shortage of pack animals, so those that the Italians did have became overworked. Knowledge of the region was patchy even among those officers who had been in Africa for months. One complained: 'Having no maps or sketches, we based our calculations solely on the information obtained from an ill-organized [intelligence] service of natives, of whom we knew little or nothing, and who in the opinion of most people were merely Abyssinian spies, munificently paid by us.' Ethiopians of both sexes were a common sight in the camps and forts, welcomed for the food and female company they offered the troops, and while the smarter men on the Italian side must have realized that many were spying for Menelik, nothing was done to keep them away.

The army was supplied with heliographs, but for some reason these were never used at Adowa (it has been suggested that the brigade commanders 'forgot' to take them forward, perhaps to allow themselves relative freedom from micro-management by Gen Baratieri). Many of the messengers sent between the separated brigades during the battle were either very slow or never made it at all. The battlefield had many farmsteads scattered about, and it is possible that some of these couriers were waylaid by local farmers – as were large numbers of the unfortunate stragglers during the final retreat.

Like all European armies, the Italians had a generally well-trained and well-equipped medical corps, but during the Adowa campaign insufficient funding led to a shortage of supplies of all kinds, and it appears that – like the commissariat – the medical corps suffered from this. Its troubles were exacerbated by the huge number of wounded and the general chaos after Adowa. In forts and rear bases, however, the Italian soldier could expect as good treatment as late 19th-century medicine could provide.

Ascari gunners practising with a Type 75B mountain gun, as used at Adowa and in most other battles of the campaign; the Native Artillery were distinguished by yellow sashes. The airburst shrapnel round of the mountain gun could be devastating, but the crews were vulnerable to skilled Ethiopian riflemen working their way forwards under cover, and at Adowa most were overrun and killed during the final rushes. The Italians enlisted Sudanese for the artillery, since they were unwilling to spread this dangerous technical skill among the population of their colony – though as it turned out, Menelik's own gun crews proved themselves fairly capable despite their lack of formal training. (Piero Crociani Collection)

Tactics

General Arimondi had developed a tactic of having reserves echeloned in rear of the main line of battle, who could come out to stop Ethiopian enveloping attacks or to counterattack weakened enemy groups. Arimondi urged his men to fight in extended line in order to reduce casualties from enemy firearms. This looser formation worked well against the Mahdist Dervishes, but the Ethiopians had better weapons and were better marksmen. In any case, newly arrived officers without battlefield experience tended to use parade-ground tactics in the field. The Italians at Adowa fought shoulder to shoulder in close formation, providing good targets for skilled Ethiopian riflemen. (In justice, it must be said that inadequately trained soldiers who might have trouble recognizing their officers probably should not have been deployed in loose formation anyway.)

Rifles

The Italians used a variety of rifles during their colonial adventures in East Africa. At the beginning of the colonial period they carried the 10.4mm M1870 Vetterli, a single-shot modification (on grounds of economy) of the Swiss M1869 bolt-action repeater. By the time of the Adowa campaign they had introduced the M1870/87 Vetterli-Vitali, an Italian modification with a box magazine holding four rounds.

Sources differ over whether any of the Italian troops at Adowa used the Army's latest weapon, the 6.5mm M1891 Carcano with a six-round box magazine, although it had arrived in Eritrea. A shortage of its new smokeless-powder ammunition (and the unwillingness of the cash-strapped Italian government to order more) meant that M1891s were actually collected from some of the reinforcements destined for Africa, and replaced with older types for which there was more ammunition in stock. Some Italian troops seem to have been issued not even with Vetterlis, but with old 'rolling-block' Remingtons left over from a previous generation. These were of both Italian

Native Brigade (General Albertone)

1st Native Battalion (Maj Turitto)	950 rifles
6th Native Bn (Maj Cossu)	850 rifles
7th Native Bn (Maj Valli)	950 rifles
8th Native Bn (Maj Gamerra)	950 rifles
Irregulars:	
Oluke-Kusai & Hamacen	
bands (Lts Sapelli & De Luca)	376 rifles
Artillery:	
1st Native Battery (Capt Henri)	4 guns
2nd Section/2nd Mtn Bty (Lt Vibi)	2 guns
3rd Mtn Bty (Capt Bianchini)	4 guns
4th Mtn Bty (Capt Masotto)	4 guns
Totals:	4,076 rifles, 14 guns

1st Infantry Brigade (General Arimondi)

1st Bersaglieri Regiment (Col Stevani):	
1st Bn (Maj De Stefano)	423 rifles
2nd Bn (LtCol Compiano)	350 rifles
2nd Infantry Regiment (Col Brusati):	
2nd Inf Bn (Maj Viancini)	450 rifles
4th Inf Bn (Maj De Amicis)	500 rifles
9th Inf Bn (Maj Baudoin)	550 rifles
Attached:	
1st Co/5th Native Bn (Capt Pavesi)	220 rifles
Artillery:	
8th Mtn Bty (Capt Loffredo)	6 guns
11th Mtn Bty (Capt Franzini)	6 guns
Totals:	2,493 rifles, 12 guns

2nd Infantry Brigade (General Dabormida)

3rd Infantry Regiment (Col Ragni):	
5th Inf Bn (Maj Giordano)	430 rifles
6th Inf Bn (Maj Prato)	430 rifles
10th Inf Bn (Maj De Fonseca)	450 rifles

6th Infantry Regiment (Col Airaghi):	
3rd Inf Bn (Maj Branchi)	430 rifles
13th Inf Bn (Maj Rayneri)	450 rifles
14th Inf Bn (Maj Solaro)	450 rifles
Attached:	
Native Mobile Militia Bn (Maj De Vito)	950 rifles
Native Kitet Co of Asmara (Capt Sermasi)	210 rifles
Artillery:	
2nd Artillery Brigade (Col Zola):	
5th Mtn Bty (Capt Mottino)	6 guns
6th Mtn Bty (Capt Regazzi)	6 guns
7th Mtn Bty (Capt Gisla)	6 guns
Totals:	3,800 rifles, 18 guns

3rd Infantry Brigade (General Ellena)

4th Infantry Regiment (Col Romero):	
7th Inf Bn (Maj Montecchi)	450 rifles
8th Inf Bn (LtCol Violante)	450 rifles
11th Inf Bn (Maj Manfredi)	480 rifles
5th Infantry Regiment (Col Nava):	
Alpini Bn (LtCol Menini)	550 rifles
15th Inf Bn (Maj Ferraro)	500 rifles
16th Inf Bn (Maj Vandiol)	500 rifles
Attached:	
3rd Native Bn (LtCol Galliano)	1,150 rifles
'Quick-Firing Gun Brigade' (Col De Rosa):*	
1st QF Bty (Capt Aragno)	6 guns
2nd QF Bty (Capt Mangia)	6 guns
Engineer half-company	70 rifles
Totals:	4,150 rifles, 12 'quick-firers'

Grand totals: 14,519 rifles, 44 guns, 12 'quick-firers'

* Note: It is unclear from the sources whether 'quick-firers' refers to mountain guns or some kind of automatic weapons.

and Egyptian licence-built models differing in small details, some dating back to the army of the Papal States and the years before unification. The Remington was an extremely sturdy and simple weapon, but some had been poorly stored and proved unreliable. Another problem was that troops trained on bolt-action magazine rifles found the action unfamiliar and cumbersome, and this slowed down their rate of fire on a battlefield where sustained rapid fire became vital.[2]

Artillery

At Adowa the Italians had 56 Type 75B light mountain guns organized into ten batteries. These 75mm brass-barrelled breech-loaders fired either high explosive or shrapnel shells fused for air burst or impact, and also had a canister round. They had an effective range of 4,200 yards, and were well-suited for campaigning in the Horn of Africa; they could be disassembled easily, with the barrel, wheels, trail, and ammunition packed

---

2 With a bolt-action magazine rifle, the firer lifts, pulls back, then pushes forwards and down the handle of a sliding cylindrical bolt at the breech; this mechanically ejects the empty cartridge case, feeds a new round into the chamber, and re-cocks the action. The Remington 'rolling block' system requires him to cock a big external hammer, then grip a small protruding thumb-pad to rotate a breechblock backwards; this jerks back a section of the chamber lip, half-ejecting the old cartridge, which he then pulls out with his fingers and replaces with a new round, before closing the re-cocked action once more.

onto four mules. Their drawback was that they were a carriage-recoil piece (rather than having recoiling barrels), so they had to be laid again after each shot. At Adowa they proved effective in the early stages of the battle, but were later silenced by Ethiopian 'pom-poms', which had greater accurate range. While a number of Italian 'home guard' (reservist) crews were shipped out with the 1896 reinforcements, most crews were ascari from the Sudan. A battery officially consisted of four Italian officers, 11 Italian NCOs or gunners, and 163 ascari serving five or six guns, but in the field a 'battery' could be as small as three guns.

It is unclear whether the Italians had automatic weapons at Adowa, although photos show Gardner machine guns in Eritrea. There are numerous references to two batteries of 'quick-firers' in Ellena's reserve, but at that date this Italian term could refer to either conventional pieces or automatic weapons. While the reference to 56 guns may thus refer to 44 mountain guns and 12 automatic weapons, the latter, if present, were in any case not brought into use until the Italians had already been routed.

SELECT BIBLIOGRAPHY

Abreha, Aseffa, 'The Battle of Adwa: Victory and its Outcome' in *Adwa: Victory Centenary Conference* (Institute of Ethiopian Studies, Addis Ababa University, 1998) pp.129–181

Adugna, Minale, 'The Role of Women during the Campaign of Adwa' in *Adwa Victory Centenary Conference Proceedings* (Michigan State University, East Lansing, 1996) pp.12–25

Berkeley, G.F.H., *The Campaign of Adowa and the Rise of Menelik* (A. Constable, Westminster, 1935)

Berhe, Hiluf, *The Battlefield of Adwa and its Potential for Tourism Development* (unpublished M.A. thesis; Addis Ababa University, July 2007)

Carmichael, Tim, 'Arms for Adwa: Menilek's Acquisition of Weapons through Harar' in *Adwa Victory Centenary Conference Proceedings* (Michigan State University, East Lansing, 1996) pp.105–109

Catellani, Renzo, & Gian Carlo Stella, *Soldati d'Africa, Volume primo, 1885–1896* (Ermanno Albertelli Editore, Parma, 2002)

Chapple, David, 'The Firearms of Adwa' in *Adwa: Victory Centenary Conference* (Institute of Ethiopian Studies, Addis Ababa University, 1998) pp.47–78

Duggan, Christopher, *The Force of Destiny: A History of Italy since 1796* (Allen Lane, London, 2007)

Hailemelekot, Abebe, *The Victory at Adowa* (Commercial Printing Enterprise, Addis Ababa, 2007)

Jaffé, Hosea, 'The African Dimension of the Battle' in *Adwa: Victory Centenary Conference* (Institute of Ethiopian Studies, Addis Ababa University, 1998) pp.403–418

Kassu, Wudu Tafete, 'The Two *Wagsums* and the Battle' in *Adwa: Victory Centenary Conference* (Institute of Ethiopian Studies, Addis Ababa University, 1998) pp.221–235

Marcus, Harold, *The Life and Times of Menelik II: Ethiopia, 1844–1913* (Red Sea Press, Lawrenceville, NJ, 1995)

Marcus, Harold, *A History of Ethiopia* (University of California Press, Berkeley, 1994)

Melake, Tekeste, 'The Military Intelligence Aspect of the 1896 Battle of Adwa' in *Adwa: Victory Centenary Conference* (Institute of Ethiopian Studies, Addis Ababa University, 1998) pp.306–319

Milikias, Paulos, 'The Battle of Adwa: The Historic Victory of Ethiopia over European Colonialism' in *Adwa Victory Centenary Conference Proceedings* (Michigan State University, East Lansing, 1996) pp.26–58

Rosati, Antonio, *Immagini delle Campagne Coloniali: Eritrea-Etiopia (1885–1896)* (Stato Maggiore dell'Esercito, Ufficio Storico, Rome, 2005)

Rotasso, Gianrodolfo, & Maurizio Ruffo, *L'Armamento Individuale dell'Esercito Italiano dal 1861 al 1943* (Stato Maggiore dell'Esercito, Ufficio Storico, Rome, 1997)

Ruggeri, Raffaele, 'The Battle of the Lions: Adua, 1896' in *Military Illustrated Past & Present* No.24 (London, April/May 1990)

Ruggeri, Raffaele, *Le Guerre Coloniali Italiane: 1885–1900* (EMI, Mornico Losana PV, Italy, 2003)

Sishagne, Shumet, 'The Genius of Adwa: Menelik II, Conservative Builder and Master Mobilizer' in *Adwa Victory Centenary Conference Proceedings* (Michigan State University, East Lansing, 1996) pp.68–74

Tegenu, Tsegaye, 'The Logistic Base and Military Strategy of the Ethiopian Army' in *Adwa: Victory Centenary Conference* (Institute of Ethiopian Studies, Addis Ababa University, 1998) pp.99–128

Wylde, Augustus B., *Modern Abyssinia* (Methuen, London, 1901)

PLATE COMMENTARIES

A: ETHIOPIAN LEADERS

A1: *Negus Negasti* Menelik II

The 'king of kings' wears a lion's-mane headdress – a traditional symbol of aristocracy – and a gold-embroidered crimson velvet cape over a striped silk tunic and white trousers; note that he also wears European-style ankle boots. He is armed with a Lebel M1886 repeating rifle, and carries a conical shield (*tafa,* or *gasha*) of sheet iron covered with velvet and tin, silver, copper and gold embellishments. Menelik's horse-harness also has lavish gold decorations. (From the well-known portrait by Paul Buffet, painted at Addis Ababa a few months after Adowa, and now in the Musée d'Orsay, Paris.)

A2: *Ras* Mekonnen

Menelik's cousin was governor of Harar province, and a general at Adowa. He wears a richly gold-embroidered navy-blue garment falling several inches below the knee, and slit deeply up the sides for ease when riding. Around his neck hangs an ornate silver cross in the Ethiopian style. Wrapped diagonally across his chest is a decorated cape of soft hide with hanging extensions, which is fastened at his left shoulder by a massive rectangular brooch. The cape's hanging extensions are gathered by the brooch and under a cartridge belt with rifle rounds, and a second belt supports the curved sheath of a traditional *shotel* sword. The shield is a simpler hunting type, of buffalo, hippopotamus or rhinocerous hide. (From the photo portrait by Luigi Naretti.)

B: ETHIOPIAN TROOPS

B1: Infantry swordsman

While some 80 per cent of the Ethiopian troops in 1896 had rifles, a minority carried only traditional equipment, like this warrior's curved *shotel* (shown drawn in **1a**), and relatively simple hide shield. His plain white *shamma,* typical of many Ethiopian peoples, is draped around his shoulders, over a long white *kammish* shirt-tunic slit up the sides, and trousers. Ethiopian warriors rarely wore footwear, since they were accustomed to walking barefoot over rough terrain.

B2: Infantry officer, Tigré

The lionskin headdress and cape show him to be a brave hunter, since only those who had killed a lion were allowed to wear them. (However, lesser men often wore headdresses made of the fur of a baboon – *gelada.*) The cape or *lembd* – whose appearance has been compared by some commentators to an Orthodox churchman's dalmatic – is the sign of his status as a member of the highest warrior caste; note that it incorporates at the front two wide hanging extensions of decorated leather. His primary weapon would probably be a Vetterli M1870 rifle, a reminder of friendlier times before Italy stopped arms shipments.

B3: Amhara rifleman, Shewa

The central Ethiopian kingdom of Shewa was made up of Oromo and Amhara; the people of the latter were mostly Christian, and this warrior too would wear an Ethiopian-style silver cross at his throat. He wears a simpler velvet *lembd*

A group of warriors from Eritrea in Italian service, 1896; a number of such elements were present with Baratieri's army at Adowa. There is little to distinguish them from Menelik's warriors, except perhaps for a higher proportion of modern rifles. The man standing tallest appears to be the leader, to judge from his fine robe; note his ammunition belt (see A2), and also the lionskin cape worn by the man on the right. (Courtesy SME/US)

over his plain white *shamma,* with the hanging front extensions gathered under a sash and his sword belt, and a small white turban. His weapon is a Mauser M1871 rifle. The Ethiopians generally did not use bayonets, since they were already skilled with equally effective hand-to-hand weapons.

C: SUDANESE MAHDIST WARRIORS

C1: Baqqara cavalryman

This warrior is protected by quilted armour under an iron helmet and long ringmail shirt; note too the extensive quilted horse-armour and leather chamfron. He is armed with a spear with a broad leaf-shaped head, and a *kaskara* sword and flintlock pistol carried on his saddle. The Dervishes plundered many Martini-Henry rifles from defeated Egyptian soldiers, but the only modern touch to disrupt the splendidly medieval impression created by this warrior is a holstered revolver at his hip.

C2: Sudanese footsoldier

This infantryman, too, wears quilted armour; while useless against firearms, this was still fairly effective against the spears and swords of the Mahdists' tribal enemies. He is armed with a spear, and a *kaskara* sword carried in a crocodile-skin scabbard; the flared end of the scabbard is purely stylistic, as the blade has conventional parallel edges. His concave hide shield with a large boss and nicked rim is of a type common in the Sudan.

D: ITALIAN INFANTRY, 1895–96

D1 & 2: Private, *Cacciatori d'Africa,* marching order

The first of these light infantry units was raised in 1887 specifically for service in Africa, but although a battalion served with the Eritrea garrison they did not take part in the advance to Adowa in 1896. They were distinguished by a tall green feather *panache,* rising from a pompon bearing the battalion number, on the right side of the M1887 cork helmet; this did not have a chinstrap for foot troops. Helmet badges identified the branch of service, set on a large cockade in the red, white and green of the Italian national tricolour. Apart from these branch distinctions, this soldier wears the standard Italian infantry uniform and equipment seen at Adowa. The new service jacket and trousers, authorized in 1887 but officially ordered only in February 1889, are of linen in a pale khaki shade called in Italian 'light bronze'; note that a matching cloth helmet cover was also sometimes issued. The tunic had five front buttons, shoulder straps, and two pleats down the front that gave it something of the look of a 'Norfolk jacket' (see H1); there were slight alterations to the cut in 1892 and 1893. The standing collar bore the national star of Savoy for all branches, in white cloth for rankers – here the collar is opened and folded down, hiding the badge. The regulation boots are almost covered here by light cloth spat-type gaiters to protect them from the dust and thorns.

On the eve of the Adowa campaign Gen Baratieri ordered that all his infantry be issued the M1874/81 dark blue cape of the Bersaglieri and Alpini, carried here in a horseshoe roll. The belt has two large ammunition pouches, also supported by a strap round the neck. He has an old-fashioned M1876 iron-strapped wooden water canteen, and his haversack of blue-and-white ticking material for spare underclothes and small kit dates back to the Piedmontese army (off-white haversacks were also used). The white metal lidded messtin was sometimes carried fastened to the back of the belt, containing immediate-use rations. His weapon is the old 10.4mm M1870/87 Vetterli; the new 6.5mm M1891 Mannlicher-Carcano rifle was not issued in Eritrea until summer 1896, after the Adowa campaign.

D3: Corporal, *Fanteria d'Africa*, marching order

Most of the soldiers newly arrived in the last few months before Adowa had not received the full field kit, but rather a variety of items haphazardly issued or obtained. This corporal – note the red rank insignia, worn on both forearms – has a wide-brimmed M1887 straw hat, modelled on the seaman's hat that some officers and troops of the *Corpo Speciale d'Africa* had acquired for use since 1885. This soldier has been on the march for several days; his uniform is ragged, and his boots are showing signs of wear. He carries an M1868 Remington 'rolling-block' rifle from the armouries of the Papal States (perhaps even picked up locally, since most of these were sold to Menelik in 1883–88).

E: CAVALRY

E1: Ethiopian Oromo horseman

These elite Ethiopian cavalry played an effective part in the harassing and pursuit of the broken Italian army after Adowa. He wears a goatskin cape over a simple *shamma* robe and white trousers; note the 'big toe' style of using the stirrups. His horse harness is colourfully decorated even though he is plainly dressed and equipped – with several spears and javelins, and a simple shield with an upturned rim for catching spear-points. Additional typical weapons were a *shotel* and/or a large knife, and there are mentions of riders at Adowa firing pistols. Some period photos show Ethiopians

This portrait of Alfredo Gaddi, an enlisted man of the Carabinieri, was taken in 1896, and offers a reasonable view of the standard khaki uniform of 1887 pattern, worn with a cork helmet complete with the badge and parade plume of this corps. All Italian troops were issued with the dark blue cape of the Bersaglieri, and wore it in a horseshoe roll when in the field. The national stars on the standing jacket collar are of white linen. (Courtesy SME/US)

with revolvers. Like their rifles, these would have been of a variety of makes; relatively few would have been used in battle, where a rifle was much more useful. The tough local horses and ponies were favoured for their ability to endure the punishing terrain and conditions of the highlands.

E2: *Ascari*, native cavalry 'Penne di Falco'; Kassala, 1894

This Eritrean soldier's red *tarbush* has no tassel; it is decorated with a hawk's feather, a multi-coloured striped turban, and the Italian cavalry badge of an un-numbered unit – a crowned disc bearing the Savoy cross, set on crossed lances. He wears a white jacket and trousers with buttoned cloth leggings. The red sash identifies the 2nd (Keren) Squadron, raised in 1890, which fought the Mahdists at Second Agordat and Kassala; the 1st (Asmara) Sqn, which wore a yellow/red striped sash, was raised in 1889 and disbanded in 1894. He is armed with an M1870/87 Vetterli carbine with integral bayonet, its ammunition carried in a locally-made pouch-bandolier; an M1874 revolver, with a separate cartridge belt; an M1871 cavalry sabre; and a large native knife. When items of kit wore out, individuals often replaced them with local equivalents – even the sabre was sometimes replaced with a *shotel*. He would ride a full-sized European horse; since these were unsuited to work in the Ethiopian uplands, this small unit did not fight at Adowa.

F: ITALIAN OFFICERS, 1895–96

F1: Artillery lieutenant, marching order
The small M1895 service cap – an item widely worn in the field – has a white crown, dark blue band, and black peak and chinstrap. It displays the gold-embroidered badge of his branch of service above two gold rank stripes, and at the base of the band a piping in branch-of-service colour – here, red. The officers' version of the M1887 khaki jacket had additional internal pockets (note the buttons on the pleats). The insignia are silver national stars on the collar, and the

Another posed studio portrait, showing Lt Mario Abba of the Carabinieri in parade dress, taken at Massawa in 1895. Note the blue sash worn from his right shoulder, under the bandolier; the officer's blue helmet band is just visible behind the badge. (Courtesy SME/US)

lieutenant's cuff ranking, of the same basic design as for NCOs but in blue. All officers of mounted branches wore a leather pouch belt over the left shoulder. The officers' light blue sash over the right shoulder was worn in Italy with all orders of dress, and in Africa with full dress and marching order. His M1889 revolver is out of sight on his right hip; his sword is the M1864 artillery officer's sabre.

F2: Beni Amer guide
This guide, from an Italian-allied tribe living in the borderlands of the Eritrea colony, wears a distinctive foot-long hairpin thrust into his 'afro'. His buff-coloured garment is similar to a *shamma*; unlike many peoples of the Shewa heartland, he does not wear trousers underneath. He carries a broadsword and a large hide shield slung from his shoulder, and a curved knife in a leather sheath at his side.

F3: Captain, *Fanteria d'Africa*, marching order
Since he would be mounted, his cork helmet has a chinstrap. The blue helmet band began life as a manoeuvre marking worn by all ranks, but later became the distinguishing mark of officers, especially in the field; from 1894 it was incorporated on their helmets by manufacturers. His uniform is virtually the same as that worn by F1, but since officers' clothing was privately tailored the exact shades of khaki often varied. Note the triple cuff ranking of a captain, and M1887 cloth leggings instead of riding boots. His sword is the M1888 officer's sabre for all branches of the *Corpo Speciale d'Africa*; it should have had a leather and metal scabbard, but photos habitually show them carried in the metal scabbard of previous home-service weapons. His revolver, again, is obscured here, worn holstered on the right hip, butt forwards. Various types of 10.35mm six-shot revolver were in simultaneous use by Italian officers; at Adowa the most common was the M1889 Glisenti, made in several differing models by dispersed factories. Given the very short effective range of any revolver, handguns were not much used except when the Ethiopians made their final rushes. When the fighting got desperate, some officers picked up rifles from dead privates and joined the firing line.

F4: Captain, *Cacciatori d'Africa*, full dress
The new white M1894 cork helmet incorporates the officers' blue band, and bears this branch's badge and parade plume. The new M1894 special full dress uniform for Africa was in dark blue cotton, its five front buttons centred on 'loops' of black cord frogging. Ranking moved from the cuffs to the shoulder straps – one to three silver stars for company officers, one to three gold for field officers. This elegant, lightweight garment was very popular, and photos show it widely worn in the field as a 'patrol jacket', with khaki or white trousers. This officer wears the complete uniform for a parade, with white gloves, and the same M1888 sabre as F2. His medals are the cross of a Knight of the Order of the Crown of Italy, and the African campaign medal with four clasps.

G: ASCARI, 1895–96

G1: Habab irregular
This youth has accompanied the Italian march more or less as a camp follower, but in hopes of earning his name in battle. The Habab, also known as Beja, are semi-nomadic Muslims from the southern Sudan between the Nile and the Red Sea, and tribesmen volunteered for both sides during

the Adowa campaign. Here the *shamma* is wrapped around the waist, leaving his chest bare and his right arm free. He carries a simple spear about 5ft long with a heavy, lozenge-shaped head, and his hippopotamus-hide shield is a slightly concave oval with a central boss. He also carries a camel-driver's sabre-shaped wooden stick.

G2: *Ascaro*, 2nd Eritrean Battalion 'Hidalgo'

The official term for a native infantryman was a *zaptiè*, but in practice *ascaro* was used for all African troops. The Native Battalions were known by the names of their commanders, and identified by the colour of the long, deep woollen *etaga* sash, and/or the tassel on the *tarbush*: 1st (Turitto) Bn, red; 2nd (Hidalgo), light blue; 3rd (Galliano), crimson; 4th (Toselli), black; 5th (Ameglio), 'tartan'; 6th (Cossu), green, later red/black; 7th (Valli), white, later red/light blue; 8th (Gamerra), russet. Here no sash is worn, but the *tarbush* has the light blue tassel. Sometimes a white headcloth was worn beneath the *tarbush*, and could be folded up around it. The clothing and equipment of native troops varied to some extent; this soldier has only a *shamma* around his shoulders, over the usual calf-length white *senafilo* trousers. The ammunition for his M1870/87 Vetterli-Vitalli 'special troops' rifle is carried in a simple waist bandolier.

G3: *Sciumbasi*, 6th Eritrean Battalion 'Cossu'

This senior NCO serves with one of Gen Albertone's ill-fated units, identified by his green sash and cap tassel. His rank, equivalent to a sergeant-major, is shown by the three silver stars on the *tarbush*, and the three red chevrons on both sleeves. Two stars and two chevrons, and one star and one chevron, were displayed by a *buluk-basci* (sergeant) and *muntaz* (corporal) respectively; the *ascaro* (private) had no rank insignia. On the march, this soldier has the dark blue Bersaglieri cape slung in a horseshoe roll, and behind his right and left hips respectively a leather waterskin and a haversack. Ammunition for his old single-shot M1870 Vetterli is carried in a single belly box, and a second belt supports the *shotel* that he carries for close work instead of a bayonet.

H: ITALIAN OFFICERS & NCO, 1895–96

H1: Sergeant-major, *Fanteria d'Africa*, marching order

In place of the cork helmet, this *furiere* – his rank identified by the two narrow and one wide red braids on his cuffs – chooses to wear the M1885/87 enlisted ranks' service cap. This dark blue cotton colonial version of the M1872/82 headgear has a cloth badge in the form of a red star piped white, bearing his original regimental number in white in a black circle. He wears the M1887 khaki jacket, with the M1887 white trousers specified for men serving with native troops, bloused into his ankle boots. His weapons are an old M1874 revolver and an M1833 infantry senior NCO's sabre, carried at his hips from a belt worn under the jacket. His field kit is the Bersaglieri cape, over a slung canteen.

H2: Infantry captain, *Truppe d'Africa*, service dress

Officers and men allocated to the cadres of native units continued to display the number of their parent regiment – here, a silver-embroidered crowned '93'. The M1887 service cap is very similar to the M1895 (see F1); but it bears two

Four artillery officers in 1896, one wearing M1887 khakis and three the dark blue M1894 colonial full dress uniform, all with white-topped service caps; compare with Plates F and H. They are named as Castelli, Saya, Capt Masotto and Capt Bianchini. All four died at Adowa, the last two while commanding the 3rd and 4th 'Sicilian' Mountain Batteries with Albertone's Native Brigade. (Piero Crociani Collection)

silver rank stripes, between two dark red branch-of-service stripes. The white uniform prescribed in 1887 for officers and men destined to serve with native troops has slightly different cuff ranking in chevron form, and shows clearly the officers' pocket details of the 1887 regulations. He carries a *curbash* local horse-whip.

H3: Lieutenant, *Bersaglieri*, marching order

Two battalions of Bersaglieri distinguished themselves at Adowa while serving with Gen Arimondi's brigade. This company officer wears the new white M1894 helmet complete with the officers' blue band and the badge and plumes of his branch. The M1887 khaki uniform is the same as that worn by F1 and F3, but with the trousers loose over ankle boots. Officers of this branch always retained the M1850 Bersaglieri officer's sabre.

INDEX